THE AMERICAN SIGN LANGUAGE *PUZZLE* BOOK

THE FUN WAY TO LEARN TO SIGN

JUSTIN SEGAL

Illustrations by BETTY C. MILLER, *with an introduction by* LOU FANT

Contemporary Books

Chicago   New York   San Francisco   Lisbon   London   Madrid   Mexico City
Milan   New Delhi   San Juan   Seoul   Singapore   Sydney   Toronto

Chapter 1 by Lou Fant and illustrations by Betty G. Miller from *The American Sign Language Phrase Book*. Copyright © 1994 by Lou Fant.

for

1 2 3 4 5 6 7 8 9 0   QPD/QPD   2 1 0 9 8 7 6 5 4 3

ISBN 0-07-141354-5

This book is printed on acid-free paper.

CONTENTS

INTRODUCTION

The American Sign Language Puzzle Book is designed to be used as a learning and testing tool on its own, but it can also be used as a companion to *The American Sign Language Phrase Book*, by Lou Fant (Contemporary Books). Each of the chapters in this book coincide with chapters in the other, and each of the themed puzzles uses vocabulary and ASL phrases exclusively from its designated chapter.

You will find several different types of puzzles in this book, at varying levels of difficulty. The puzzle types are as follows:

1. Alphabet puzzles   Alphabet puzzles are among the simplest in the book. An illustration for a handshape is followed by blanks indicating the number of letters for its English equivalent. Readers can either fill in the blanks outright or use the Manual Alphabet "keys" to decode the correct definition (for a guide to the Manual Alphabet, see *page 9*).

2. Scramble puzzles   Scramble puzzles are like Alphabet puzzles, except the Manual Alphabet handshapes are mixed-up. Readers must either fill in the blanks outright or decode the alphabet, then unscramble the handshapes to get the correct fingerspelled definition (unscrambled answer: COLD).

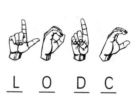 

3. Definition puzzles   Definition puzzles give readers three possible answers. Pick the correct sign definition to solve the puzzle (answer: WHERE?).

A. Up

B. One

C. Where?

4. Pyramid puzzles   Pyramid puzzles present sign illustrations and an empty "pyramid" indicating a 2-letter word sits atop a 3-letter word atop a 4-letter word, etc. Readers must determine its corresponding English equivalent that matches the sign and fill in the appropriate blanks to complete the pyramid. The signs are grouped in no particular order and the words do not add up to make a sentence.

5. Match puzzles   Match puzzles challenge readers to "match" pairs of signs that belong together (answer: HUSBAND + WIFE).

6. Search puzzles   There will be two kinds of search puzzles: in the first, readers must solve the sign definitions, then search for the sign's corresponding English equivalent in the grid. Definitions are spelled out vertically, horizontally, diagonally, forward, or backward (answers: EAT, FINISH, NOON, BABY). In the second version, the grid is comprised of Manual Alphabet handshapes.

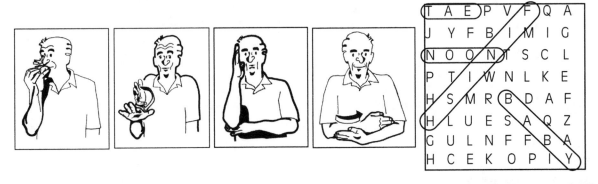

7. Crossword puzzles   To complete crosswords, solve the sign definitions, then fill in the numbered blanks in the grid.

8. Phrase puzzles   Phrase puzzles use a sequence of sign illustrations to construct ASL phrases. Readers must solve the sign illustrations, then select the appropriate signs and place them in correct syntax (sign order) to complete the puzzle.

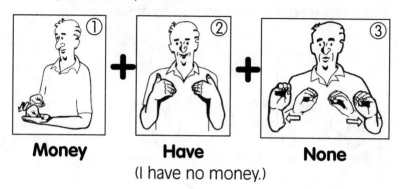

Money   **Have**   **None**

(I have no money.)

It was with sadness that I learned of Lou Fant's passing on June 11, 2001. Many thanks go to Barbara Bernstein, his widow, and to Betty G. Miller for kind permission to use her illustrations. Thanks also to Christopher Brown, my editor, as well as John Maucere and Patty Drasin, who have labored to teach me American Sign Language.

I hope you enjoy solving these puzzles as much as I have enjoyed creating them.

Justin Segal
March 2003

1 READING THE SIGNS

American Sign Language, commonly abbreviated to ASL, is the sign language most deaf people use when they are communicating among themselves. It has its own grammatical structure, which differs from English grammar. You must approach ASL in the same manner you would approach any foreign language — do not expect ASL to be like English or to conform to rules of English grammar.

It is a common misconception that ASL is merely the fingerspelling of English words. Fingerspelling — using the manual alphabet *(see page 9)* to spell out entire words letter by letter — is occasionally incorporated into ASL, but the vocabulary of ASL consists of signs. Each sign has been given a name, or label. We use English words for these labels. People often confuse the meaning of a sign with its label, but a sign may have several meanings and the label is only one of its meanings.

The pictures are to be read from left to right. An individual sign may sometimes require more than one picture to illustrate it. Several types of aids are provided to help you know which way to read a drawing, and thus form the sign correctly:

1. Dark-lined & light-lined drawings Some signs use both *bold* (dark-lined) and *light-lined* drawings. The bold-lined drawings show the final position of the sign. The light-lined drawings show the first and, if necessary, additional positions of the sign. In the sign labeled DELICIOUS (Fig. 1), for example, the light-lined drawing shows the middle finger touching the lips, The bold-lined drawing shows the hand turned outward. These are the first and final postions, respectively. Always remember that the bold-lined drawing shows the final position of the sign.

Fig. 1: DELICIOUS

2. Arrows The second aid is the use of several kinds of *arrows*, which show exactly how the hands move in forming a sign. The sign DAY (Fig. 2), for example, is formed by moving the arm from the first position (light-lined) to the final position (bold-lined), following the movement indicated by the arrow.

Fig. 2: DAY

Fig. 3: HAPPY

Repetitive movement is shown by the use of a bent arrow, as in the sign HAPPY (Fig. 3). This means you do the same movement twice.

Swerving movement is shown by a twisted arrow, as in the sign NEVER (Fig. 4).

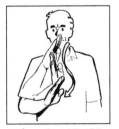
Fig. 4: NEVER

Circular movement is shown by a circular arrow, as in the sign COFFEE (Fig. 5).

Fig. 5: COFFEE

The arrows in the sign CAR (Fig. 6) show the hands repeating a move-ment, but in opposite directions. The sign looks as if you were steer-ing a car. In the sign WHICH (Fig. 7), the arrows indicate that the hands move alternately. As the left hand goes up, the right hand goes down. Then both hands reverse their directions.

Fig. 6: CAR

Fig. 7: WHICH

The *squiggles* in Fig. 8 (WAIT) are a third aid, and they tell you to wriggle the fingers.

Fig. 8: WAIT

3. The angle of the pictures　In most of the drawings the signer is shown facing directly front, but many signs can best be learned by seeing the sign from an angle slightly off-center; thus, the signer is sometimes shown from facing slightly to his right or to his left (see Fig. 9, WANT). When you make the sign, however, do not turn to your right, but make it straight toward the person to whom you are signing.

Fig. 9: WANT

4. Labeling of the drawings　When more than one drawing is required to illustrate how a single sign is made, each part of the sign is followed by a number. For example, the illustration of the sign AWFUL (Fig. 10) requires two steps, and these are labeled (1) and (2).

Fig. 10: AWFUL

5. Facial expressions　We have given our cartoon character various facial expres-sions to emphasize the importance of facial expres-sions in ASL. The expressions are by no means the same all the time. The same sign will require different expressions at different times, depending upon the feeling you wish to convey.

2 THE MANUAL ALPHABET

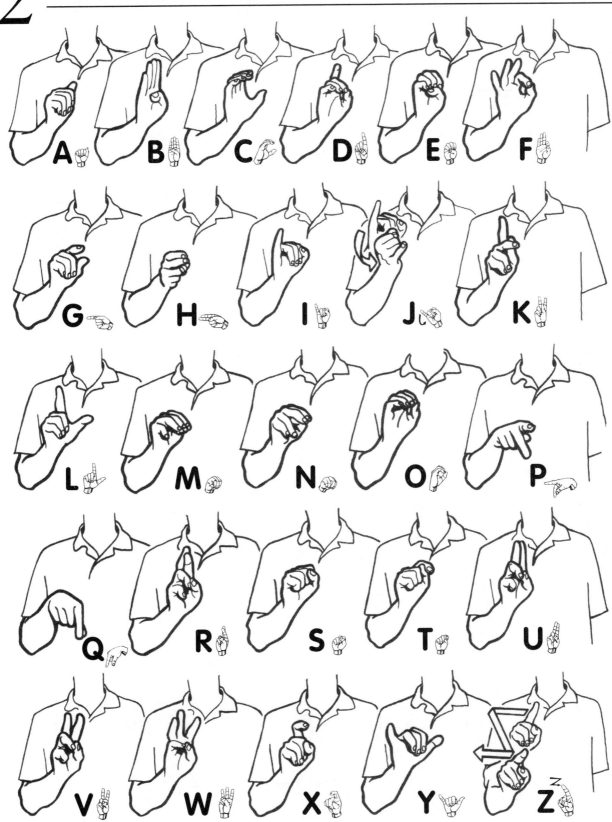

3 EVERYDAY EXPRESSIONS

ALPHABET PUZZLE

To solve the puzzle, either fill in the blanks with the correct definition or decode the Manual Alphabet key. *Answers on page 130.*

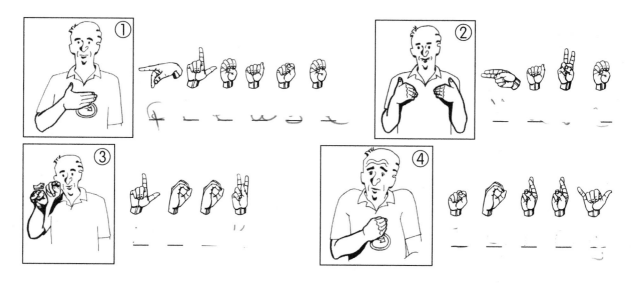

MATCH PUZZLE

Match the pairs of signs that belong together.

Answers on page 130.

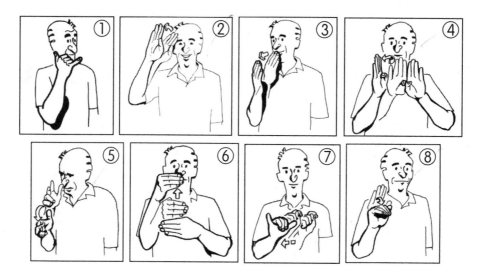

SCRAMBLE PUZZLE

To solve the puzzle, either fill in the blanks with the correct definition or decode the Manual Alphabet key, then unscramble the letters to spell the correct definition.
Answers on page 130.

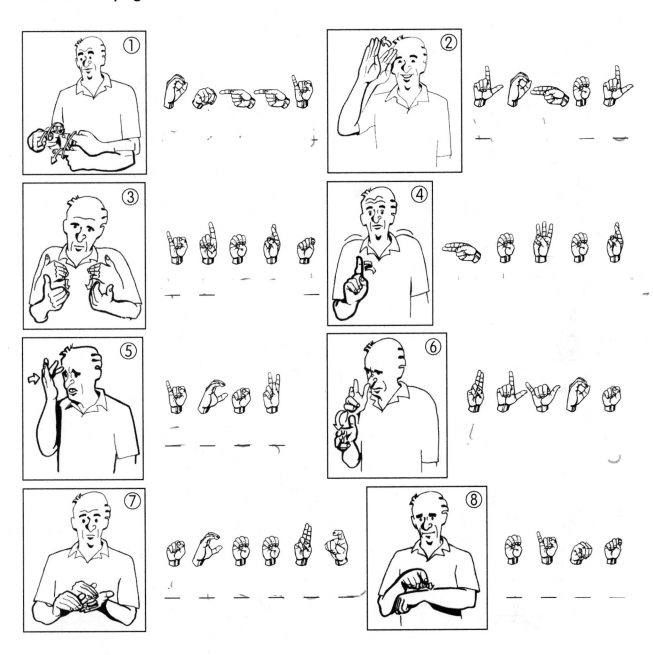

DEFINITION PUZZLE

To solve the puzzle, pick the correct sign definition. ***Answers on page 130.***

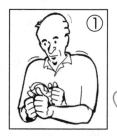

① A. To
B. For
C. With

② A. Sooner
B. Later
C. Now

③ A. A lot
B. Some
C. None

④ A. Number
B. Letter
C. Symbol

⑤ A. Fine
B. Mine
C. Combine

⑥ A. Know
B. Think
C. Feel

⑦ A. Tried
B. Tiered
C. Tired

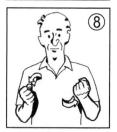

⑧ A. Truck
B. Car
C. Bus

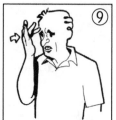

⑨ A. Sick
B. Trick
C. Thick

⑩ A. Health
B. Head
C. Home

PYRAMID PUZZLE

Solve the sign definitions, then fill in the blanks in the pyramid. The signs are grouped in no particular order and the words do not add up to make a sentence. *Answers on page 131.*

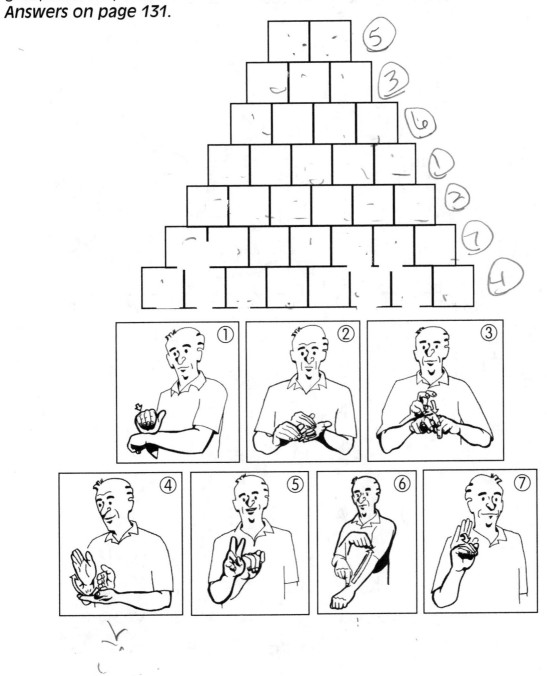

SEARCH PUZZLE

To complete the puzzle, solve the sign definitions, then search for its corresponding English equivalent in the grid. Definitions are spelled out vertically, horizontally, diagonally, forward, or backward. **Answers on page 131**.

PHRASE PUZZLE

Choose signs from the vocabulary list, then put them in the correct order to form the ASL phrases below. *Answers on page 131.*

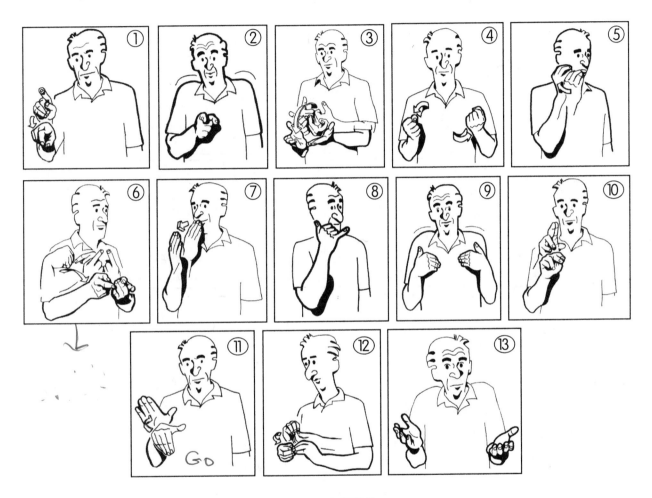

PHRASES

A. How have you been?

B. What's your phone number?

C. I have to go home.

D. How are you?

E. No, thank you.

F. Do you have a car?

CROSSWORD PUZZLE

Solve the sign definitions, then fill in the numbered blanks in the grid.
Answers on page 131.

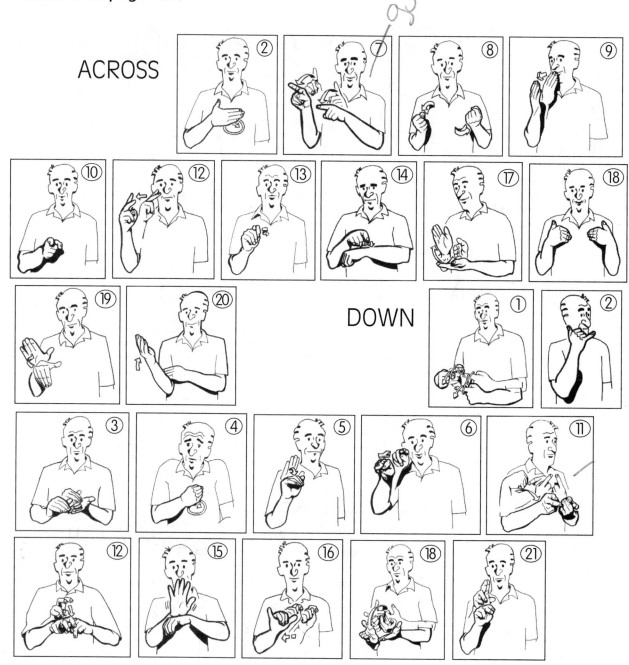

4 SIGNING and DEAFNESS

ALPHABET PUZZLE

To solve the puzzle, either fill in the blanks with the correct definition or decode the Manual Alphabet key. *Answers on page 132.*

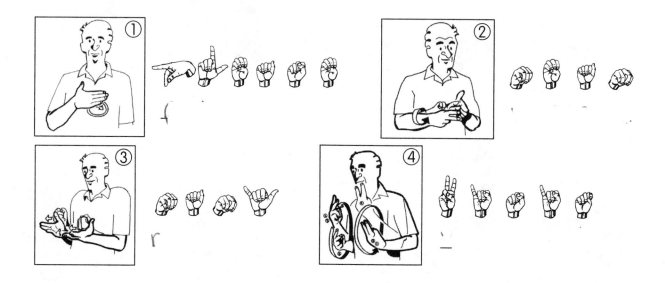

MATCH PUZZLE

Match the pairs of words that belong together.   *Answers on page 132.*

2,8
3,5

1,7

4,6

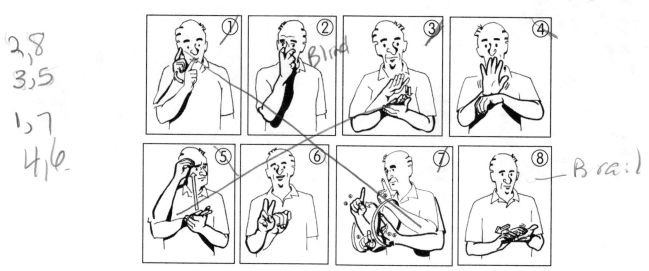

SCRAMBLE PUZZLE

To solve the puzzle, either fill in the blanks with the correct definition or decode the Manual Alphabet key, then unscramble the letters to spell the correct definition.
Answers on page 132.

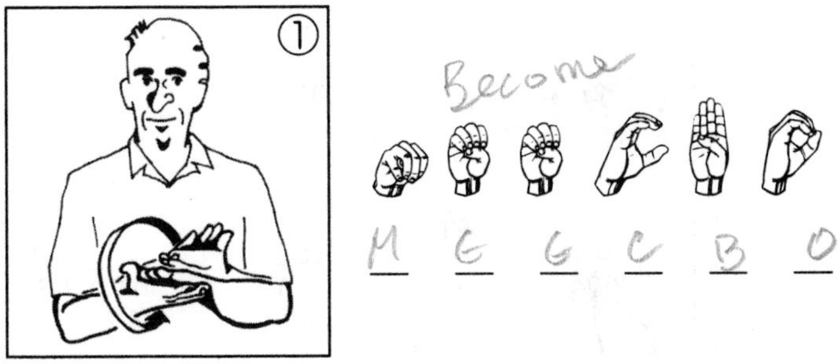

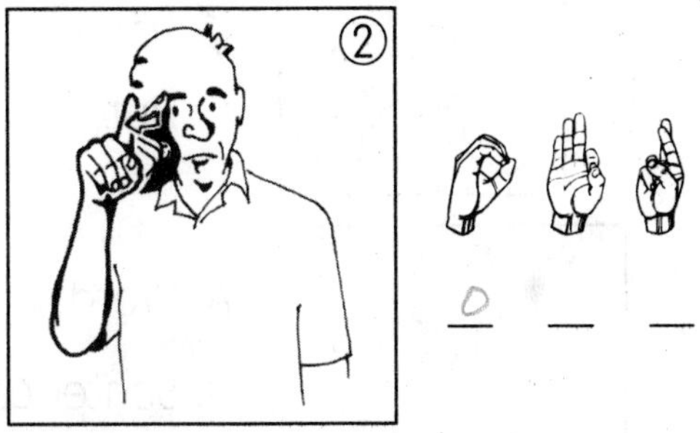

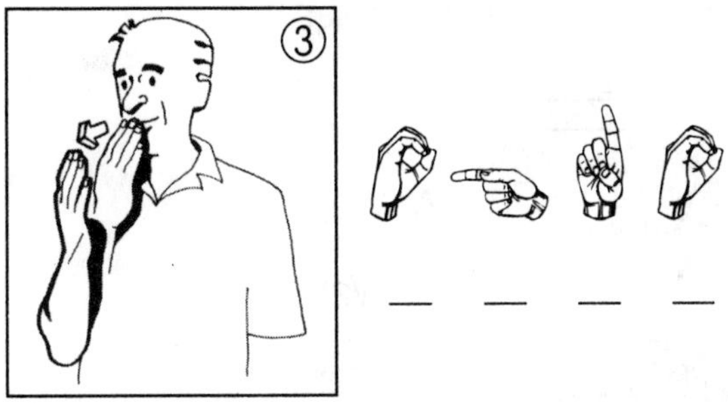

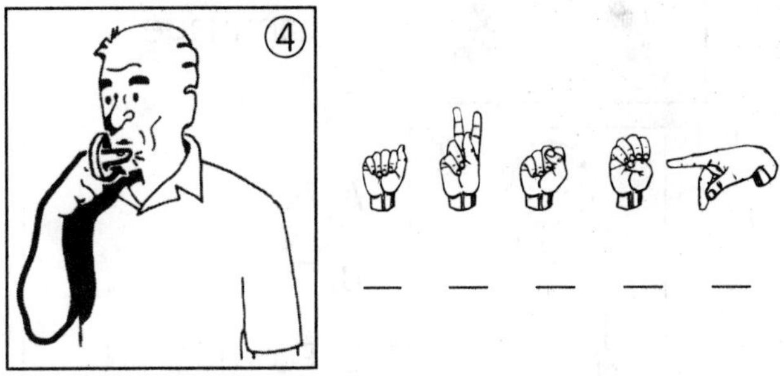

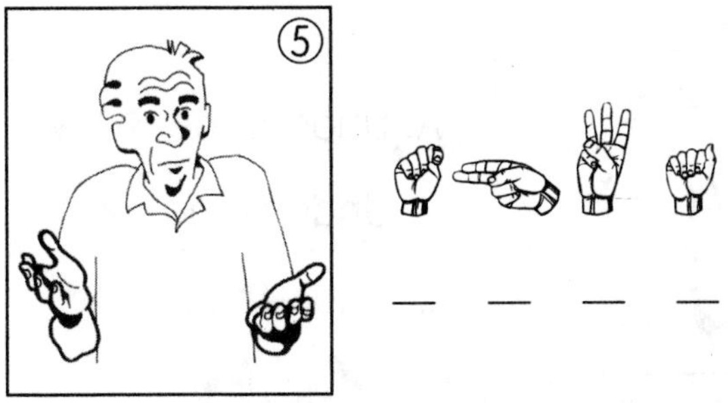

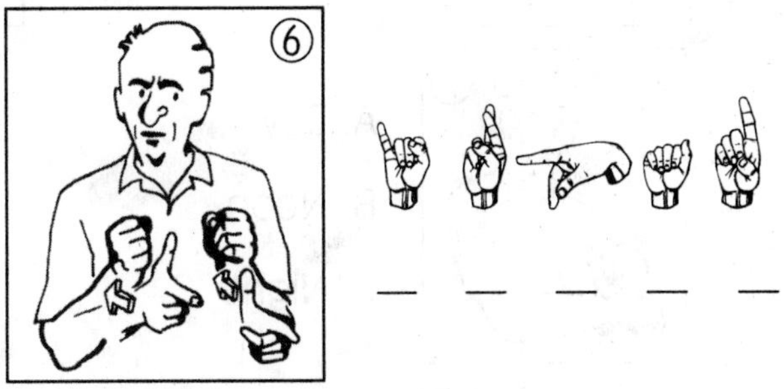

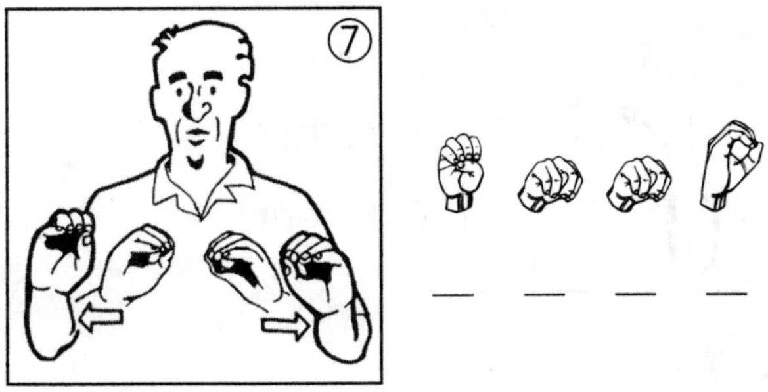

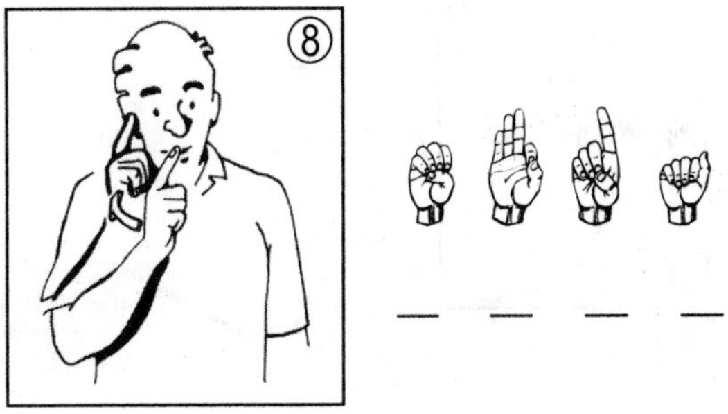

DEFINITION PUZZLE

To solve the puzzle, pick the correct word definition. *Answers on page 132.*

① A. Bit
B. Bet
C. But

② A. Choose
B. Lose
C. Shoes

③ A. Word
B. Sentence
C. Language

④ A. Past
B. Pest
C. Post

⑤ A. For
B. Form
C. Fortune

⑥ A. Wait
B. Want
C. Went

⑦ A. Day
B. Noon
C. Night

⑧ A. Underdone
B. Understand
C. Underfoot

⑨ A. Got
B. Hot
C. Not

⑩ A. Mother
B. Father
C. Parent

PYRAMID PUZZLE

Solve the word definitions, then fill in the blanks in the pyramid. The signs are grouped in no particular order and the words do not add up to make a sentence. **Answers on page 133.**

SEARCH PUZZLE

To complete the puzzle, solve the word definitions, then search for words in the grid. Definitions are spelled out vertically, horizontally, diagonally, forward, or backward.
Answers on page 133.

PHRASE PUZZLE

Choose words from the vocabulary list, then put them in the correct order to form the ASL phrases below. *Answers on page 133.*

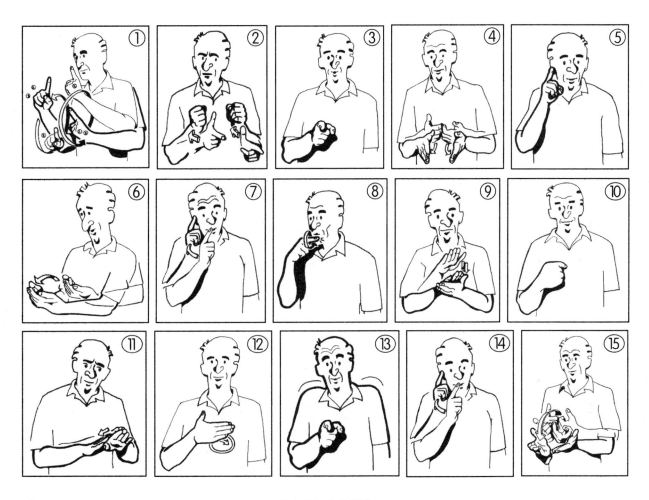

PHRASES

A. I was born deaf.

B. You sign fast.

C. How did you lose your hearing?

D. I went to a school for hearing children.

E. Are you deaf?

F. Sign slowly, please.

CROSSWORD PUZZLE

Solve the word definitions, then fill in the numbered blanks in the grid.
Answers on page 133.

5 GETTING ACQUAINTED

ALPHABET PUZZLE

To solve the puzzle, either fill in the blanks with the correct definition or decode the Manual Alphabet key. *Answers on page 134.*

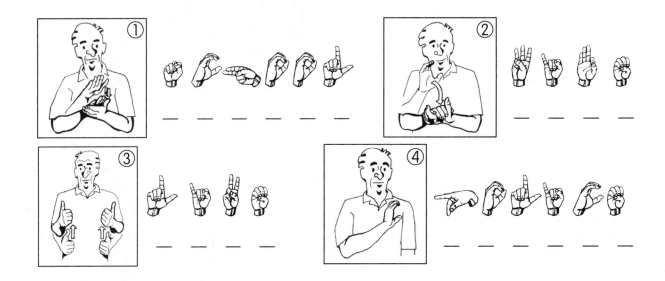

MATCH PUZZLE

Match the pairs of words that belong together.

Answers on page 134.

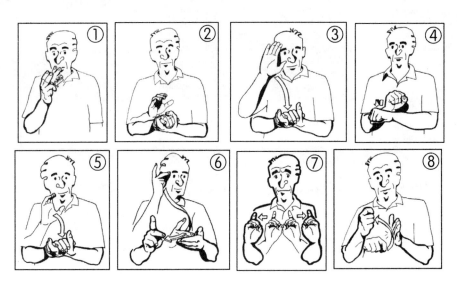

SCRAMBLE PUZZLE

To solve the puzzle, either fill in the blanks with the correct definition or decode the Manual Alphabet key, then unscramble the letters to spell the correct definition.
Answers on page 134.

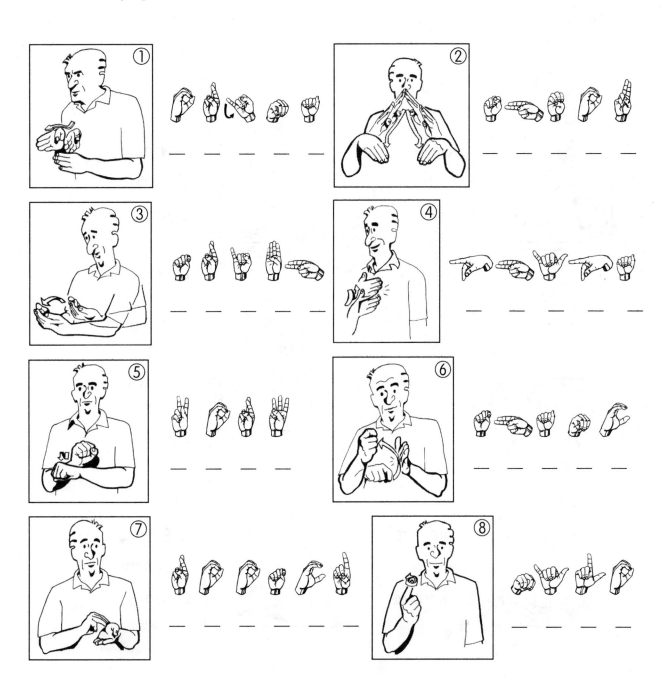

DEFINITION PUZZLE

To solve the puzzle, pick the correct word definition. ***Answers on page 134.***

A. Friend

B. Fend

C. Fired

A. Bold

B. Cold

C. Old

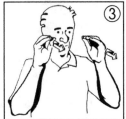

A. Reach

B. Each

C. Teach

A. Name

B. Game

C. Same

A. Policeman

B. Firefighter

C. Soldier

A. Aft

B. Art

C. Act

A. Have

B. Heave

C. Heavy

A. Law

B. Low

C. Allow

A. Interfere

B. Introduce

C. Interpret

A. Parent

B. Daughter

C. Son

PYRAMID PUZZLE

Solve the word definitions, then fill in the blanks in the pyramid. The signs are grouped in no particular order and the words do not add up to make a sentence. *Answers on page 135.*

SEARCH PUZZLE

To complete the puzzle, solve the word definitions, then search for words in the grid. Definitions are spelled out vertically, horizontally, diagonally, forward, or backward.
Answers on page 135.

PHRASE PUZZLE

Choose words from the vocabulary list, then put them in the correct order to form the ASL phrases below. **Answers on page 135.**

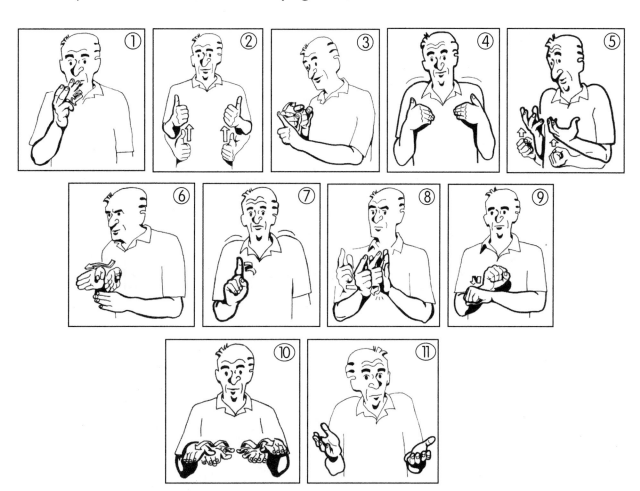

PHRASES

A. Where are you from?

B. Where do you live?

C. Where do you work?

D. What kind of work do you do?

E. How many children do you have?

F. Smoking is not allowed.

CROSSWORD PUZZLE

Solve the word definitions, then fill in the numbered blanks in the grid.
Answers on page 135.

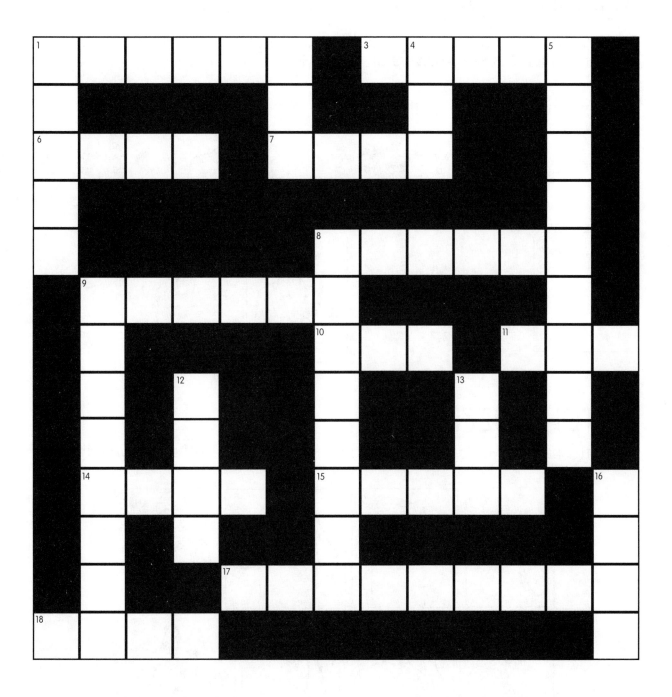

HEALTH

ALPHABET PUZZLE

To solve the puzzle, either fill in the blanks with the correct definition or decode the Manual Alphabet key. *Answers on page 136.*

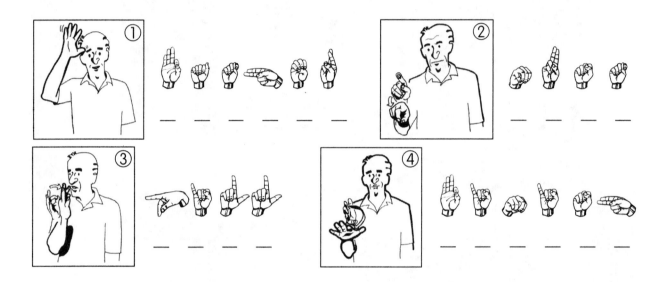

MATCH PUZZLE

Match the pairs of words that belong together.

Answers on page 136.

SCRAMBLE PUZZLE

To solve the puzzle, either fill in the blanks with the correct definition or decode the
Manual Alphabet key, then unscramble the letters to spell the correct definition.
Answers on page 136.

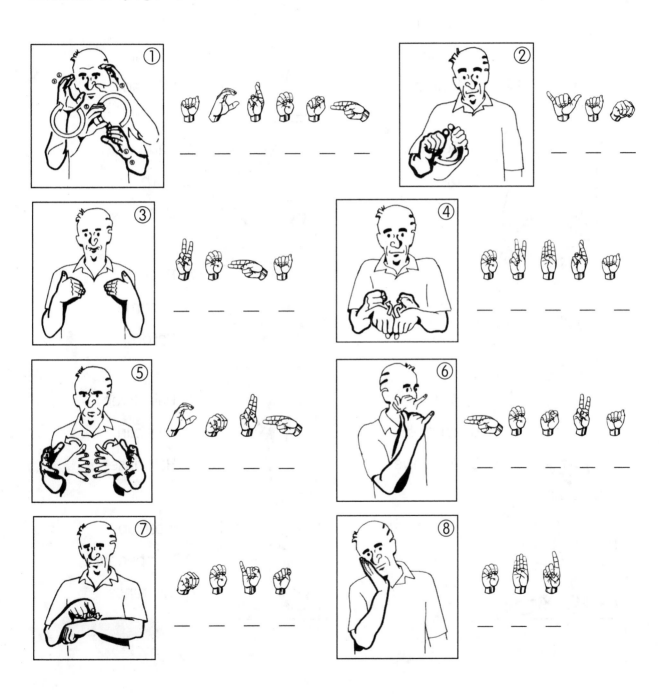

DEFINITION PUZZLE

To solve the puzzle, pick the correct word definition. *Answers on page 136.*

A. Which?

B. Why?

C. Where?

A. All over

B. All right

C. All ready

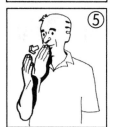

A. Born

B. Die

C. Live

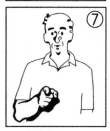

A. Bath

B. Both

C. Berth

A. Gold

B. Glad

C. Good

A. Beckon

B. Become

C. Before

A. You

B. Yourself

C. Yourselves

A. Hair dryer

B. Hair curl

C. Hair rinse

A. Next week

B. Last week

C. First week

A. Interrupt

B. Independent

C. Insurance

PYRAMID PUZZLE

Solve the word definitions, then fill in the blanks in the pyramid. The signs are grouped in no particular order and the words do not add up to make a sentence.
Answers on page 137.

SEARCH PUZZLE

To complete the puzzle, solve the word definitions, then search for words in the grid. Definitions are spelled out vertically, horizontally, diagonally, forward, or backward. **Answers on page 137.**

E X T B W O U S E D U P O
H T S U G S I D L E T Q U
S O S D N A H H S A W A R
U P T I L N O W F C S I D
R U R N Z Y J O I Z B E R
B I R F X O A M X I R B A
H A J H Y E R C H S U E W
T R E T T E B Y N I S G B
O F S O D X O H I N H A L
O S T O M A C H A C H E O
T Z P A S H R S P Y A M O
B Y P N Q A F H A R I L D
H U E S O N Y N N U R E W

PHRASE PUZZLE

Choose words from the vocabulary list, then put them in the correct order to form the ASL phrases below. **Answers on page 137.**

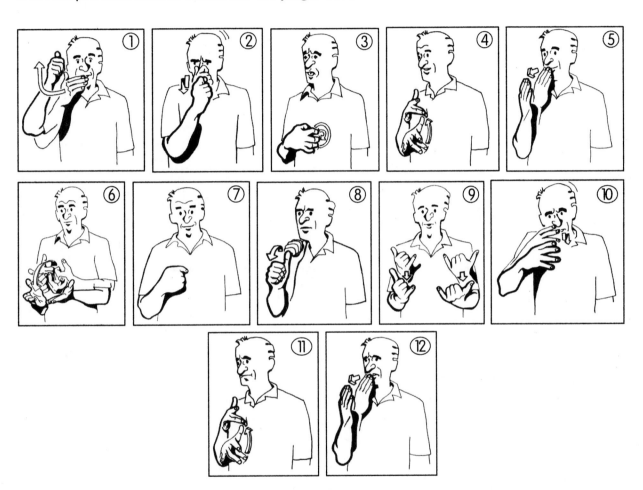

PHRASES

A. How do you feel?

B. I don't feel well.

C. I feel better now.

D. I have a cold.

E. My nose is runny.

F. My stomach is upset.

CROSSWORD PUZZLE

Solve the word definitions, then fill in the numbered blanks in the grid.
Answers on page 137.

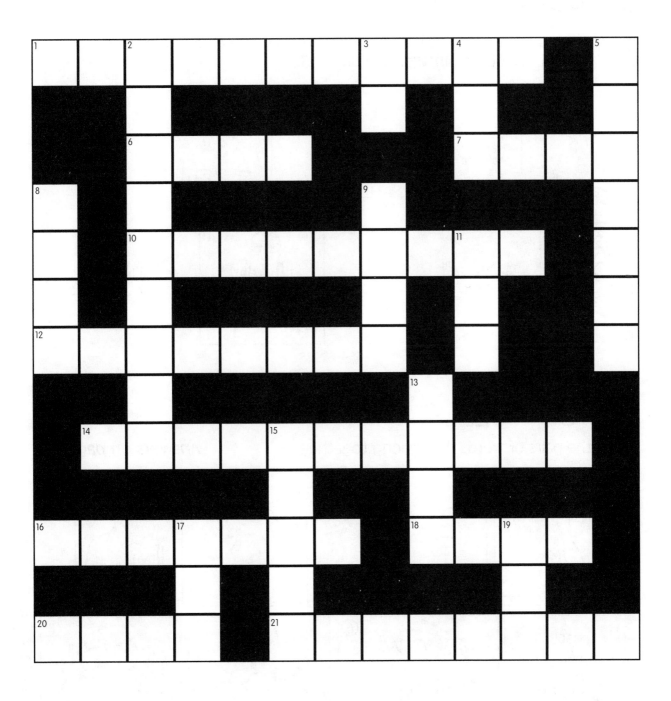

7 — WEATHER

ALPHABET PUZZLE

To solve the puzzle, either fill in the blanks with the correct definition or decode the Manual Alphabet key. *Answers on page 138.*

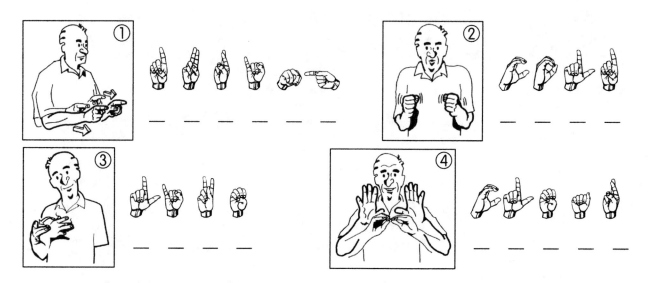

MATCH PUZZLE

Match the pairs of words that belong together.   *Answers on page 138.*

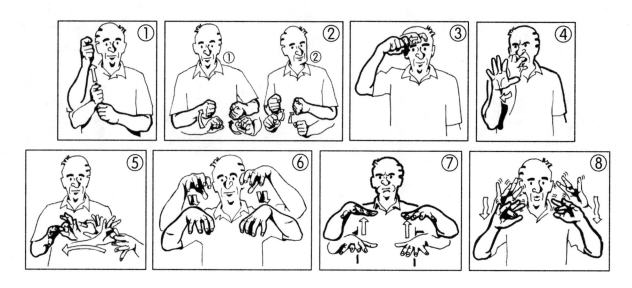

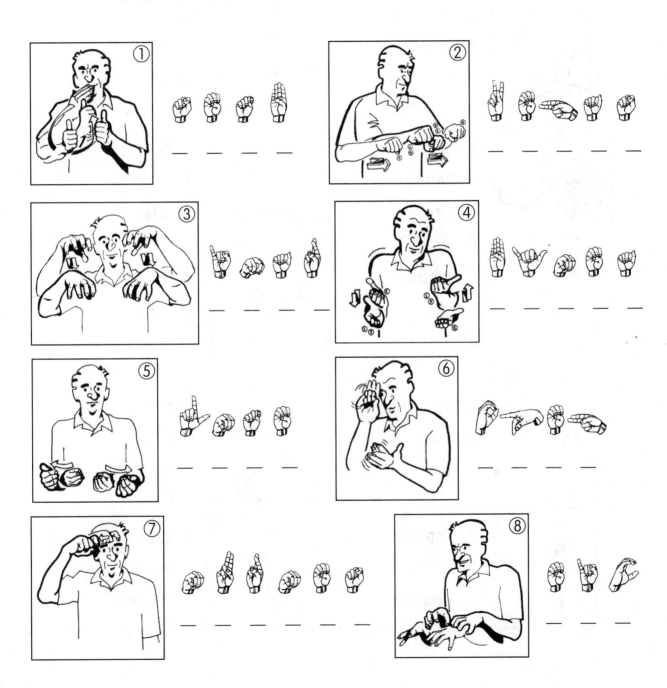

SCRAMBLE PUZZLE

To solve the puzzle, either fill in the blanks with the correct definition or decode the Manual Alphabet key, then unscramble the letters to spell the correct definition.
Answers on page 138.

DEFINITION PUZZLE

To solve the puzzle, pick the correct word definition. *Answers on page 138.*

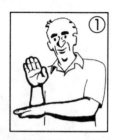

A. Morning

B. Afternoon

C. Night

A. Show

B. Slow

C. Grow

A. Sunset

B. Sunrise

C. Sunday

A. Before

B. During

C. After

A. Lightning

B. Lighting

C. Lighter

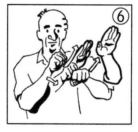

A. Launch

B. Ramp

C. Mountain

A. Last

B. Past

C. Fast

A. Require

B. Have

C. Sell

A. Yesterday

B. Today

C. Tomorrow

A. Rubber

B. Runner

C. Rudder

PYRAMID PUZZLE

Solve the word definitions, then fill in the blanks in the pyramid. The signs are grouped in no particular order and the words do not add up to make a sentence.
Answers on page 139.

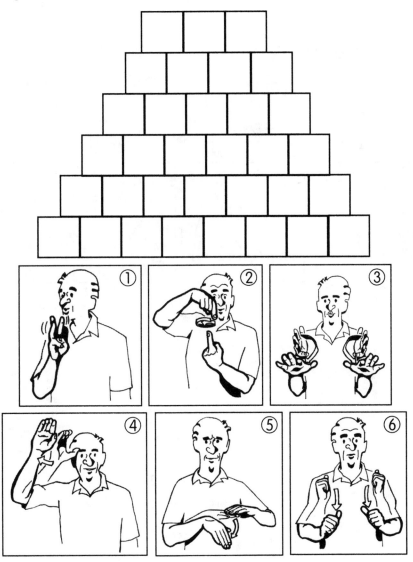

SEARCH PUZZLE

To complete the puzzle, solve the word definitions, then search for words in the grid. Definitions are spelled out vertically, horizontally, diagonally, forward, or backward.
Answers on page 139.

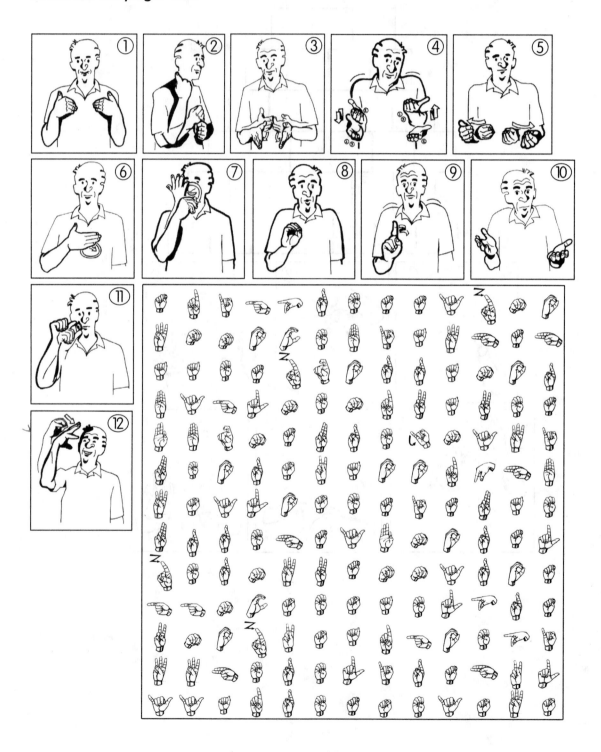

PHRASE PUZZLE

Choose words from the vocabulary list, then put them in the correct order to form the ASL phrases below. *Answers on page 139.*

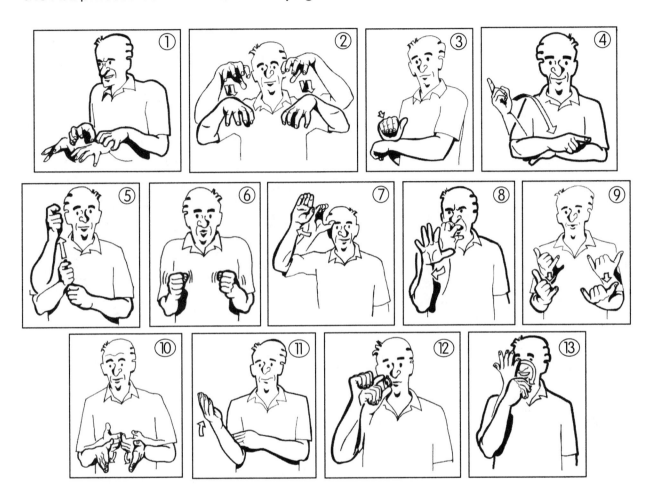

PHRASES

A. It's beautiful today.

B. It was cold this morning.

C. It will freeze tonight.

D. It rained yesterday.

E. I lost my umbrella.

F. The sun is hot.

CROSSWORD PUZZLE

Solve the word definitions, then fill in the numbered blanks in the grid.
Answers on page 139.

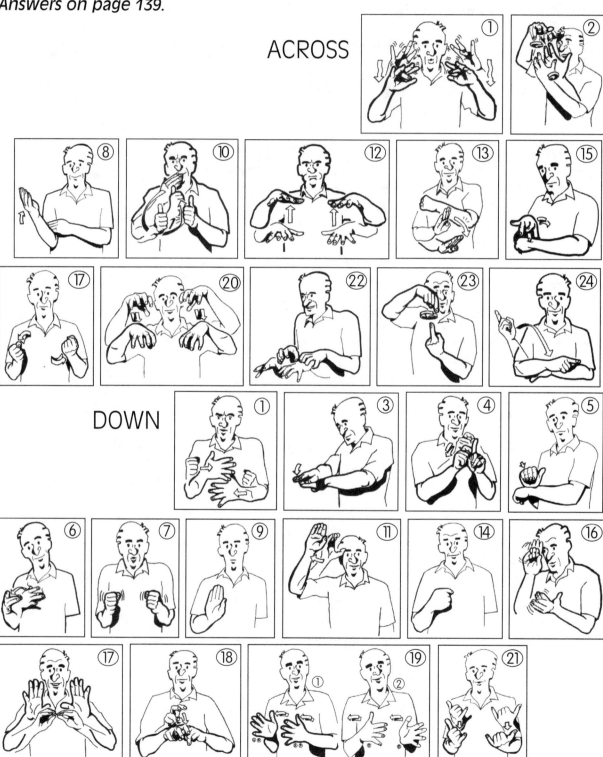

ACROSS

DOWN

FAMILY

ALPHABET PUZZLE

To solve the puzzle, either fill in the blanks with the correct definition or decode the Manual Alphabet key. *Answers on page 140.*

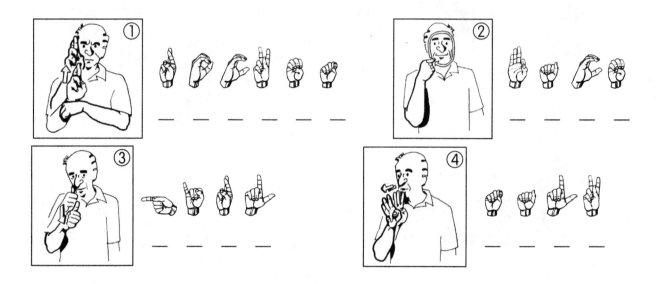

MATCH PUZZLE

Match the pairs of words that belong together.

Answers on page 140.

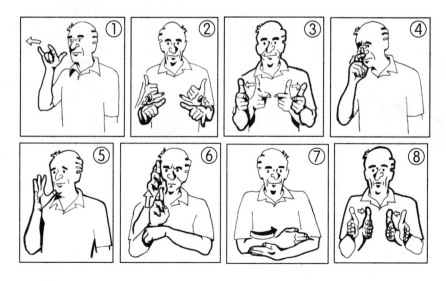

SCRAMBLE PUZZLE

To solve the puzzle, either fill in the blanks with the correct definition or decode the Manual Alphabet key, then unscramble the letters to spell the correct definition.
Answers on page 140.

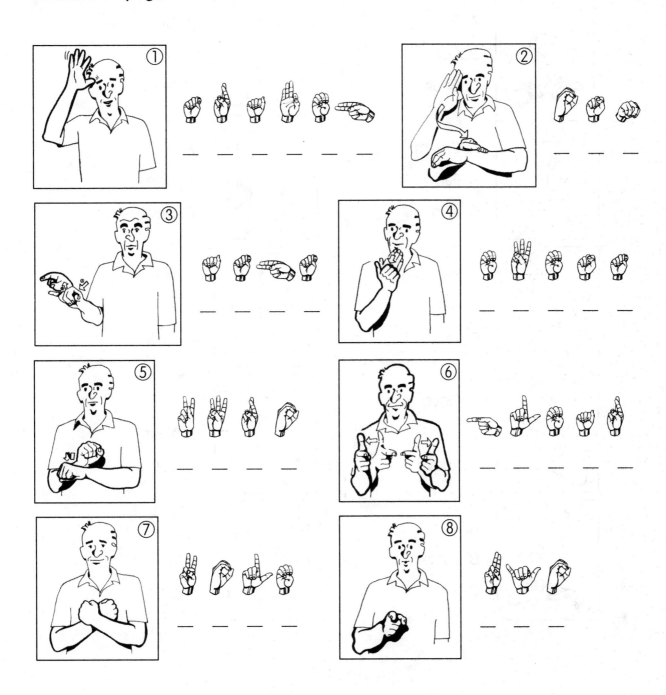

DEFINITION PUZZLE

To solve the puzzle, pick the correct word definition. *Answers on page 140.*

 ①
A. Took
B. Cook
C. Book

 ②
A. Break
B. Shake
C. Make

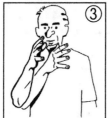 ③
A. Charm
B. Farm
C. Arm

 ④
A. Live
B. Give
C. Sieve

 ⑤
A. Yell
B. Sell
C. Tell

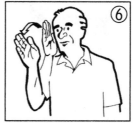 ⑥
A. Will
B. Fill
C. Chill

 ⑦
A. Glove
B. Love
C. Above

 ⑧
A. You
B. Your
C. Yourself

 ⑨
A. Slice
B. Twice
C. Nice

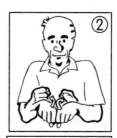 ⑩
A. Skill
B. Spill
C. Still

PYRAMID PUZZLE

Solve the word definitions, then fill in the blanks in the pyramid. The signs are grouped in no particular order and the words do not add up to make a sentence. **Answers on page 141.**

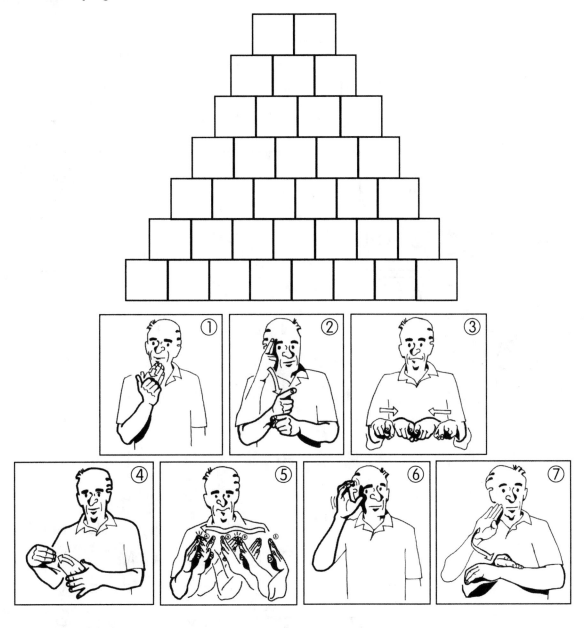

SEARCH PUZZLE

To complete the puzzle, solve the word definitions, then search for words in the grid. Definitions are spelled out vertically, horizontally, diagonally, forward, or backward. **Answers on page 141.**

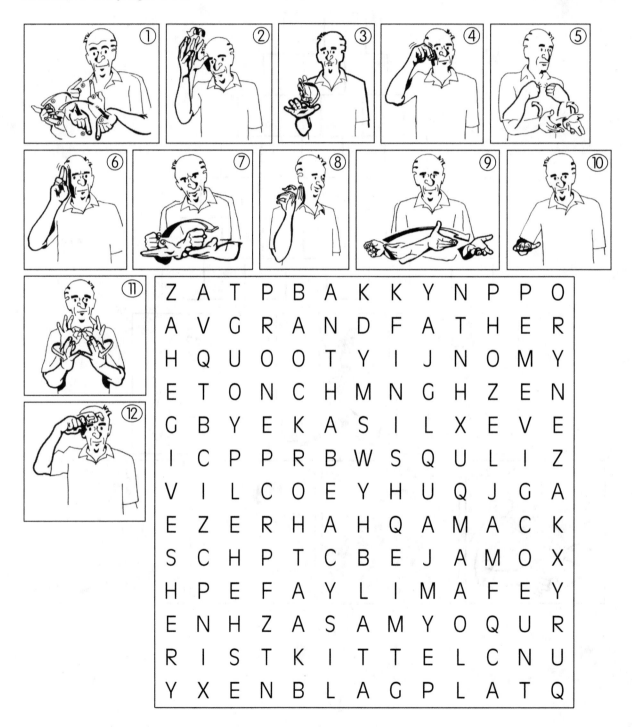

```
Z A T P B A K K Y N P P O
A V G R A N D F A T H E R
H Q U O O T Y I J N O M Y
E T O N C H M N G H Z E N
G B Y E K A S I L X E V E
I C P P R B W S Q U L I Z
V I L C O E Y H U Q J G A
E Z E R H A H Q A M A C K
S C H P T C B E J A M O X
H P E F A Y L I M A F E Y
E N H Z A S A M Y O Q U R
R I S T K I T T E L C N U
Y X E N B L A G P L A T Q
```

PHRASE PUZZLE

Choose words from the vocabulary list, then put them in the correct order to form the ASL phrases below. *Answers on page 141.*

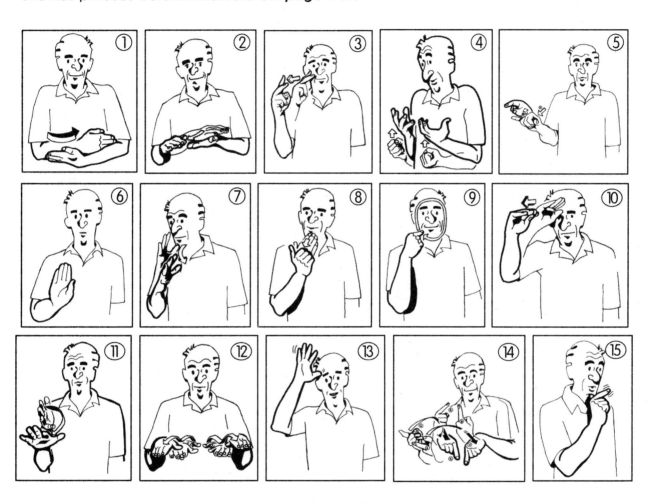

PHRASES

A. The baby is cute.

B. Who is that man?

C. Did you see the woman?

D. How many children are coming?

E. Your father is nice looking.

CROSSWORD PUZZLE

Solve the word definitions, then fill in the numbered blanks in the grid.
Answers on page 141

ACROSS

DOWN

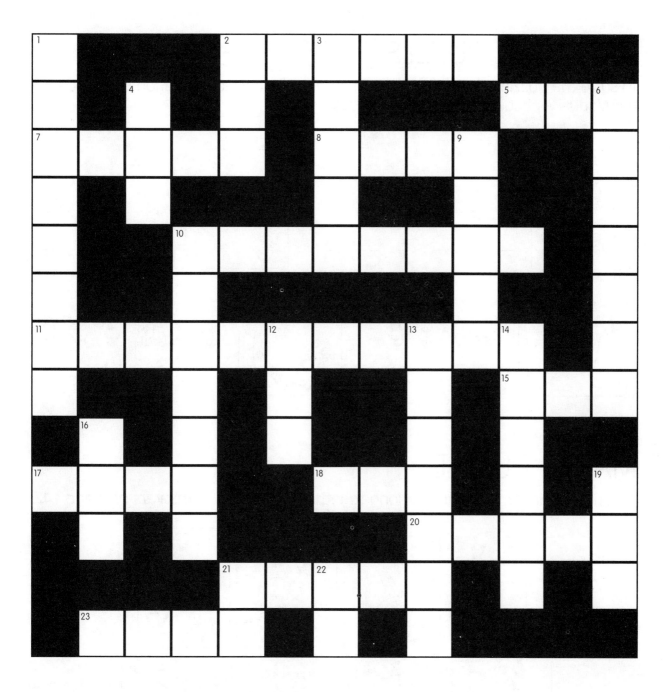

9   SCHOOL

ALPHABET PUZZLE

To solve the puzzle, either fill in the blanks with the correct definition or decode the Manual Alphabet key. *Answers on page 142.*

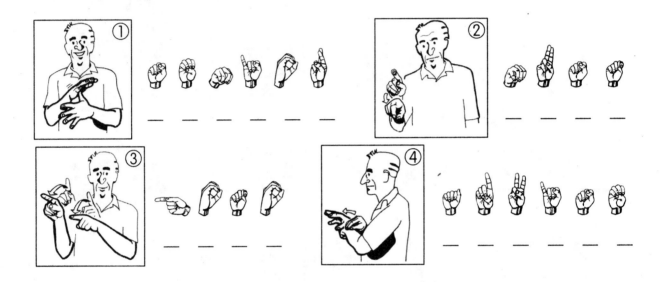

MATCH PUZZLE

Match the pairs of words that belong together.   *Answers on page 142.*

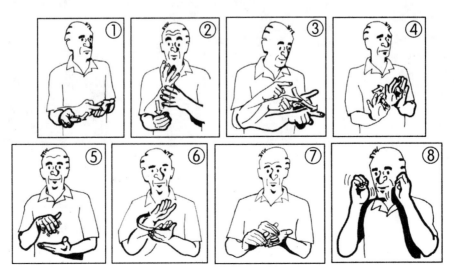

SCRAMBLE PUZZLE

To solve the puzzle, either fill in the blanks with the correct definition or decode the Manual Alphabet key, then unscramble the letters to spell the correct definition.
Answers on page 142.

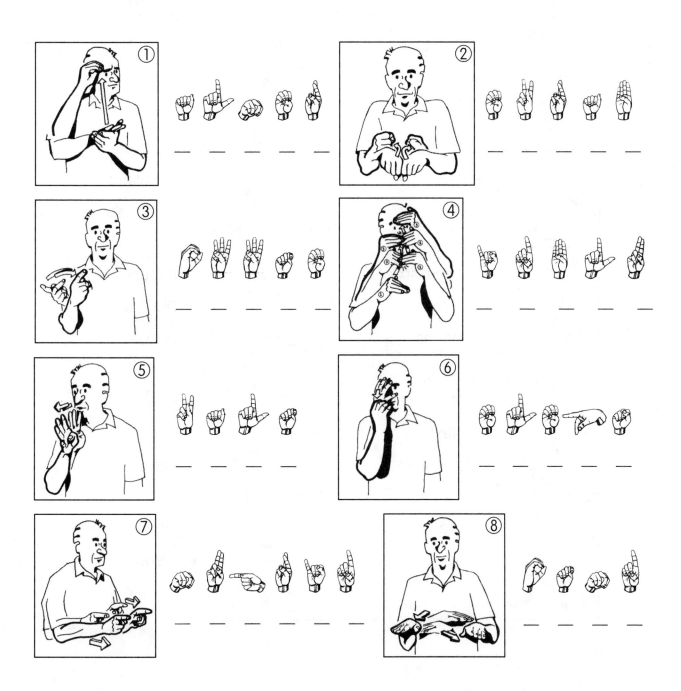

DEFINITION PUZZLE

To solve the puzzle, pick the correct word definition. ***Answers on page 142.***

① A. All night

B. All day

C. All the time

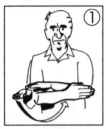

② A. Pen

B. Pencil

C. Paper

③ A. Friend

B. Lend

C. Mend

④ A. Computer

B. Calculator

C. Typewriter

⑤ A. Chemistry

B. History

C. Drama

⑥ A. Discuss

B. Dismiss

C. Discover

⑦ A. This year

B. Next year

C. Last year

⑧ A. Plus

B. Pass

C. Period

⑨ A. Week

B. Year

C. Semester

⑩ A. English

B. French

C. Spanish

PYRAMID PUZZLE

Solve the word definitions, then fill in the blanks in the pyramid. The signs are grouped in no particular order and the words do not add up to make a sentence. **Answers on page 143.**

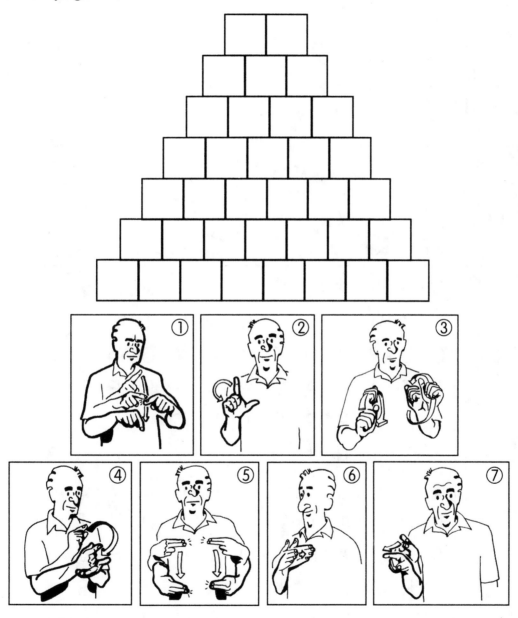

SEARCH PUZZLE

To complete the puzzle, solve the word definitions, then search for words in the grid. Definitions are spelled out vertically, horizontally, diagonally, forward, or backward.
Answers on page 143.

W	E	R	A	S	E	B	O	A	R	D	Z	M
A	X	W	O	R	R	O	M	O	T	E	E	T
C	O	R	Y	U	O	Z	A	X	O	Y	A	O
A	T	A	N	A	M	H	S	E	R	F	P	N
L	A	N	R	P	O	L	Y	T	I	E	X	E
C	T	I	B	I	H	O	R	P	N	E	O	Z
U	Y	N	Z	I	P	N	R	B	E	M	O	W
L	P	H	I	L	O	S	O	P	H	Y	T	E
A	A	T	A	H	S	O	T	O	A	R	M	J
T	R	A	N	I	K	O	N	K	R	E	S	T
O	E	G	E	E	L	B	A	S	V	U	V	E
R	H	F	U	U	G	I	T	I	U	Q	U	E
Z	T	U	Q	N	E	A	G	X	E	L	E	P

PHRASE PUZZLE

Choose words from the vocabulary list, then put them in the correct order to form the ASL phrases below. **Answers on page 143.**

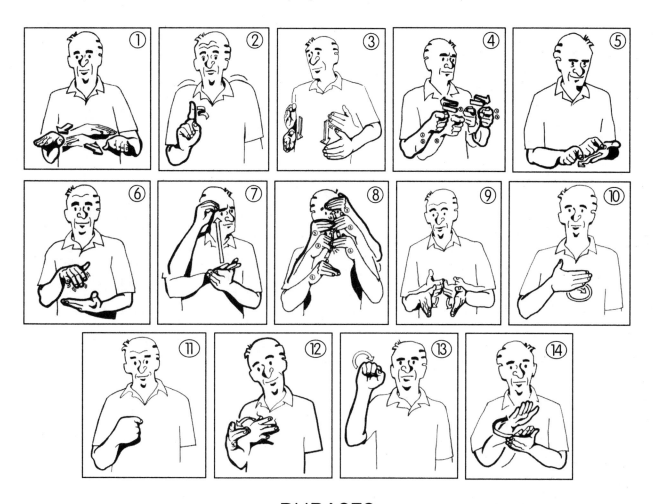

PHRASES

A. I lost my pencil.

B. Where's the administration building?

C. I'm a student.

D. I like to study.

E. I go to college.

F. Please don't erase the board.

CROSSWORD PUZZLE

Solve the word definitions, then fill in the numbered blanks in the grid.
Answers on page 143.

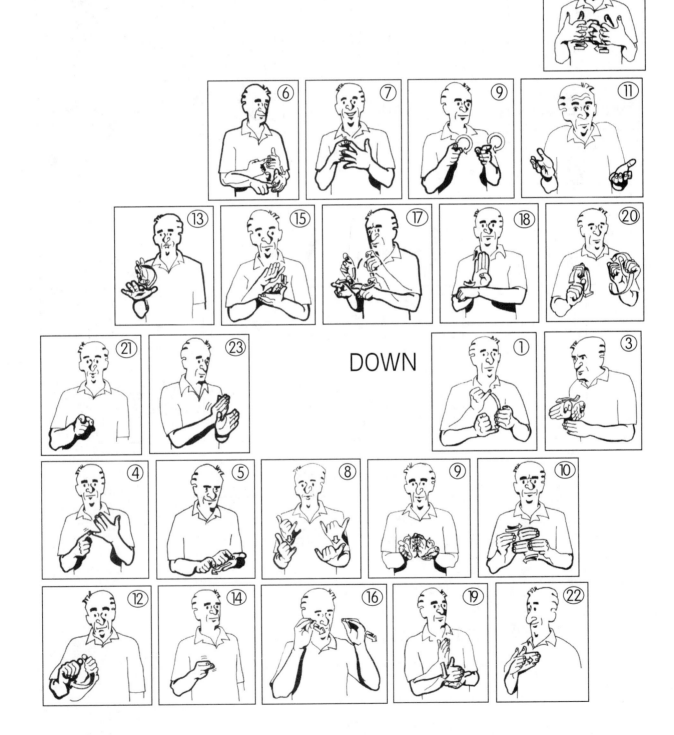

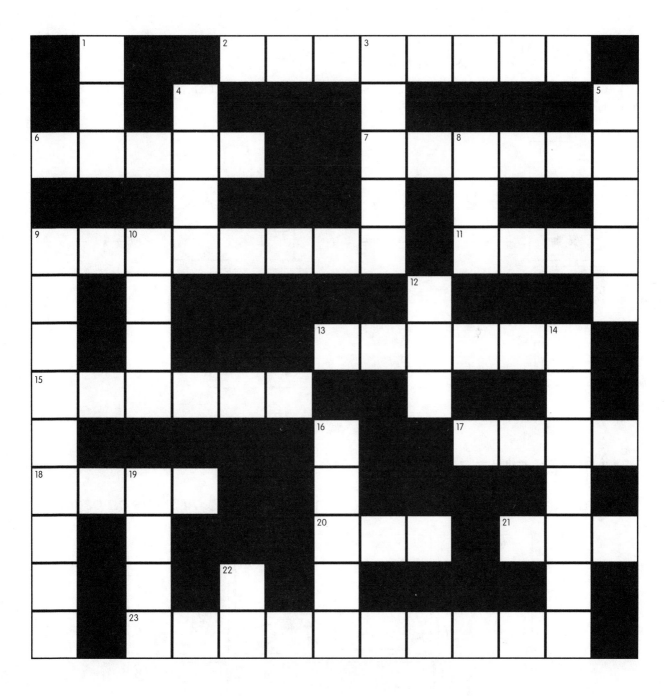

10 — FOOD and DRINK

ALPHABET PUZZLE

To solve the puzzle, either fill in the blanks with the correct definition or decode the Manual Alphabet key. *Answers on page 144.*

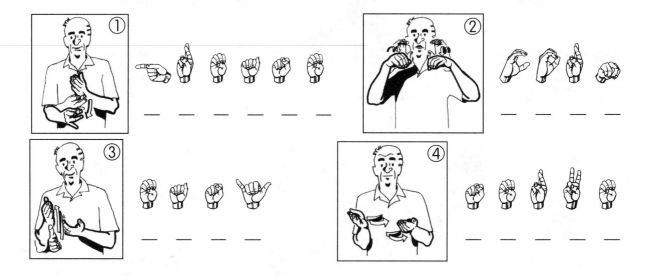

MATCH PUZZLE

Match the pairs of words that belong together.

Answers on page 144.

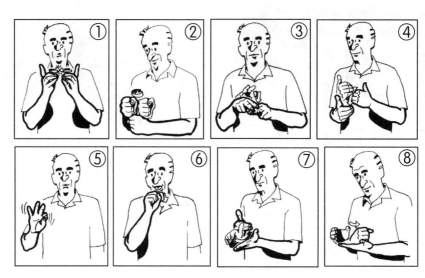

SCRAMBLE PUZZLE

To solve the puzzle, either fill in the blanks with the correct definition or decode the Manual Alphabet key, then unscramble the letters to spell the correct definition.
Answers on page 144.

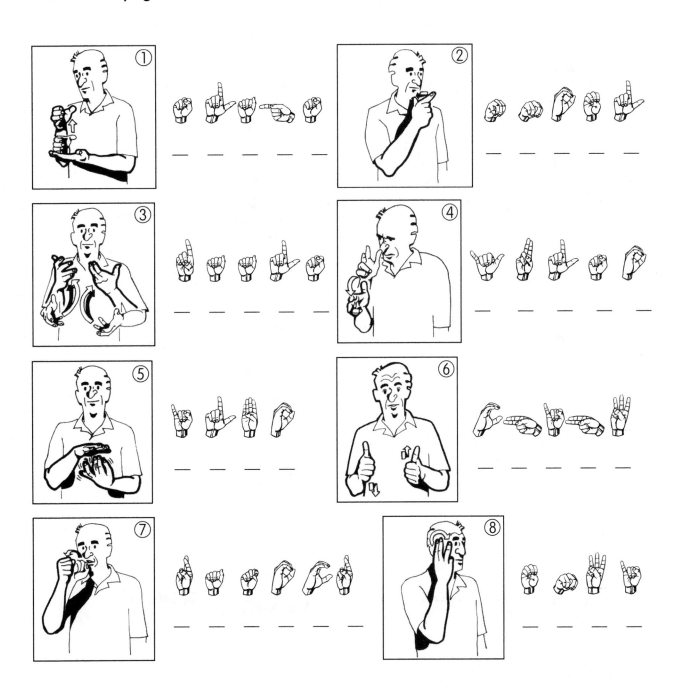

DEFINITION PUZZLE

To solve the puzzle, pick the correct word definition. **Answers on page 144.**

A. Apple

B. Peach

C. Orange

A. Water

B. Milk

C. Juice

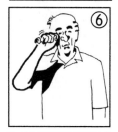

A. Whiskey

B. Wine

C. Beer

A. Bacon

B. Eggs

C. Sausage

A. Coke

B. Pepsi

C. 7-Up

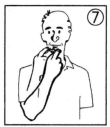

A. Pickle

B. Onion

C. Relish

A. Deli

B. Diner

C. Restaurant

A. Meat

B. Fruit

C. Vegetables

A. Fork

B. Knife

C. Spoon

A. Small

B. Medium

C. Large

PYRAMID PUZZLE

Solve the word definitions, then fill in the blanks in the pyramid. The signs are grouped in no particular order and the words do not add up to make a sentence. *Answers on page 145.*

SEARCH PUZZLE

To complete the puzzle, solve the word definitions, then search for words in the grid. Definitions are spelled out vertically, horizontally, diagonally, forward, or backward. *Answers on page 145.*

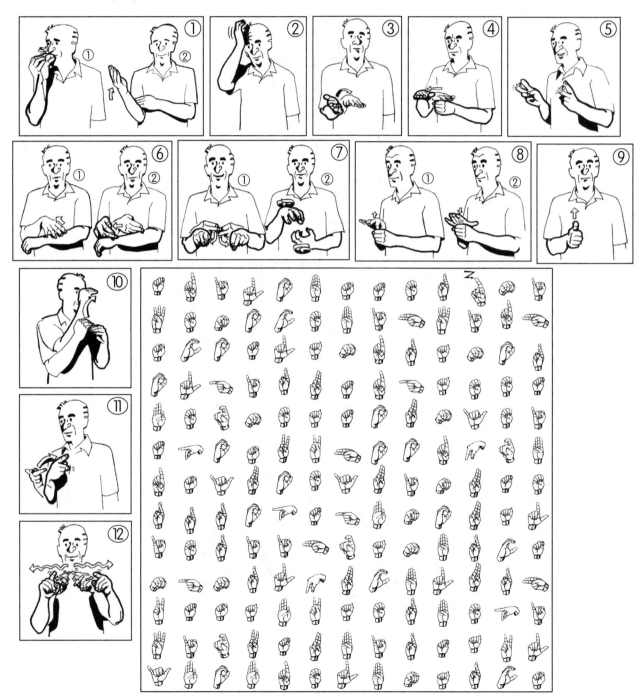

PHRASE PUZZLE

Choose words from the vocabulary list, then put them in the correct order to form the ASL phrases below. **Answers on page 145.**

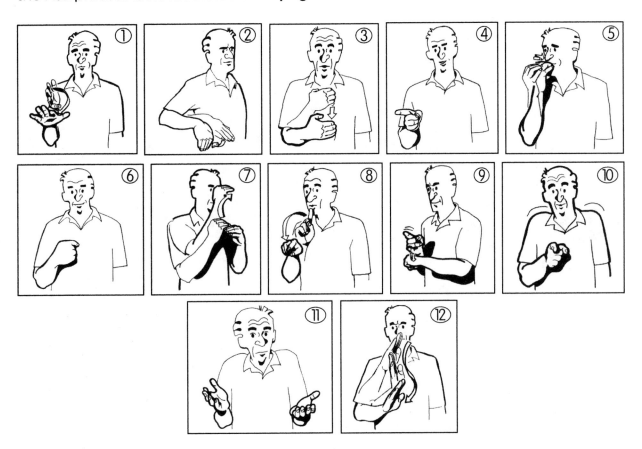

PHRASES

A. Did you eat?

B. I haven't eaten yet.

C. Are you hungry?

D. He never drinks whiskey.

E. What are you going to order?

F. He eats too much.

CROSSWORD PUZZLE

Solve the word definitions, then fill in the numbered blanks in the grid.
Answers on page 145.

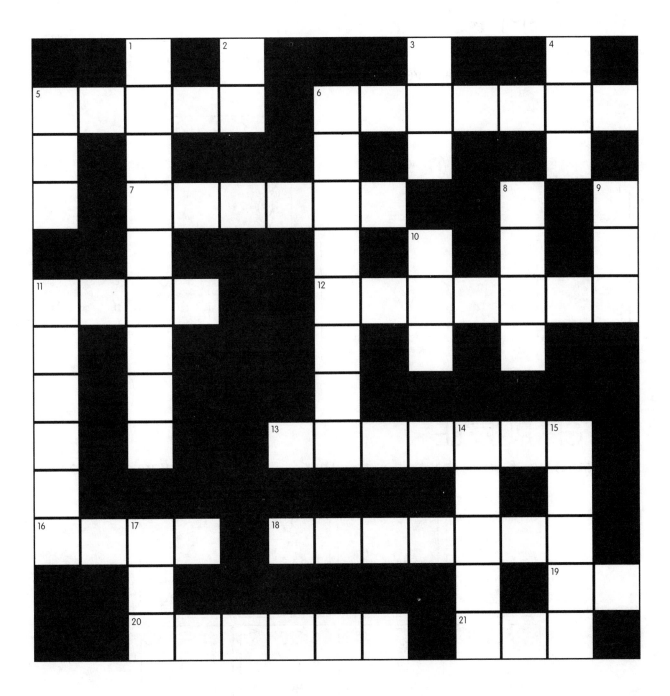

11 CLOTHING

ALPHABET PUZZLE

To solve the puzzle, either fill in the blanks with the correct definition or decode the Manual Alphabet key. *Answers on page 146*.

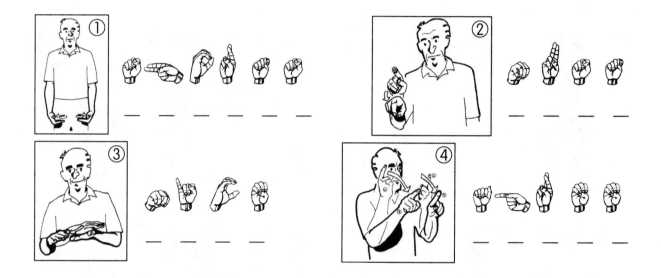

MATCH PUZZLE

Match the pairs of words that belong together.   *Answers on page 146*.

SCRAMBLE PUZZLE

To solve the puzzle, either fill in the blanks with the correct definition or decode the Manual Alphabet key, then unscramble the letters to spell the correct definition.
Answers on page 146.

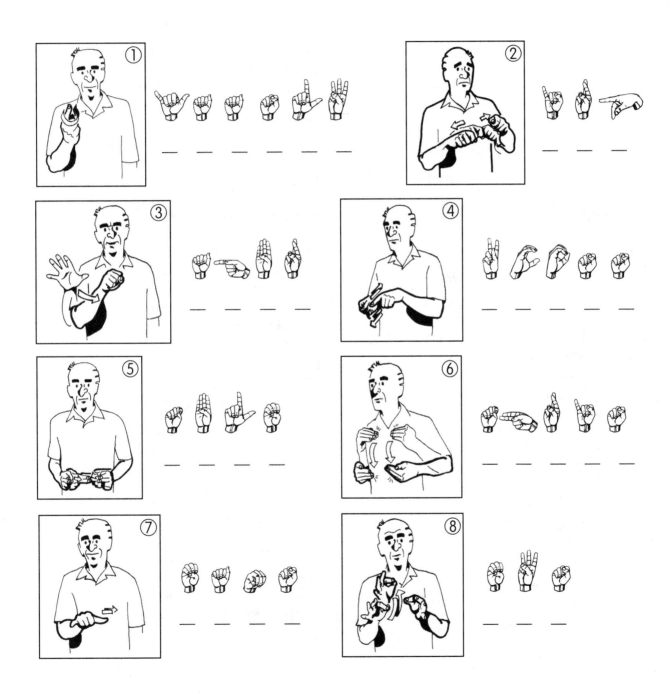

DEFINITION PUZZLE

To solve the puzzle, pick the correct word definition. ***Answers on page 146.***

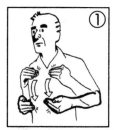

① A. Shirt

B. Coat

C. Jacket

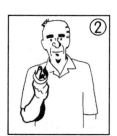

② A. Never

B. Sometimes

C. Always

③ A. Who?

B. What?

C. Why?

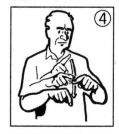

④ A. Shouldn't

B. Can't

C. Won't

⑤ A. Day

B. Noon

C. Night

⑥ A. Wrinkled

B. Faded

C. Dirty

⑦ A. Some

B. A few

C. Most

⑧ A. Begin

B. Work on

C. Finish

⑨ A. Man

B. Woman

C. Child

⑩ A. Near

B. Rear

C. Here

PYRAMID PUZZLE

Solve the word definitions, then fill in the blanks in the pyramid. The signs are grouped in no particular order and the words do not add up to make a sentence.
Answers on page 147.

SEARCH PUZZLE

To complete the puzzle, solve the word definitions, then search for words in the grid. Definitions are spelled out vertically, horizontally, diagonally, forward, or backward. **Answers on page 147.**

```
E  J  W  D  M  A  U  Q  G  N  A  R  W
A  V  E  N  A  C  N  A  U  P  Y  O  P
Q  U  E  X  E  A  Z  I  A  T  A  Y  J
V  U  R  E  L  I  M  N  J  E  D  L  W
S  K  C  A  L  S  T  M  O  D  Y  U  L
I  A  C  E  X  S  E  W  L  W  R  J  Q
W  A  L  M  E  E  R  N  O  W  E  W  U
I  D  E  A  R  W  O  E  R  B  V  E  R
G  W  A  S  H  C  L  O  T  H  E  S  E
E  F  N  E  Z  A  I  N  O  R  Z  G  I
E  Q  E  M  O  K  V  Y  O  U  O  W  H
D  U  R  I  N  G  H  E  U  Q  U  H  C
O  N  S  E  G  E  E  W  R  L  O  O  S
```

PHRASE PUZZLE

Choose words from the vocabulary list, then put them in the correct order to form the ASL phrases below. ***Answers on page 147.***

PHRASES

A. I can't fasten my belt.

B. Do you have any dirty clothes?

C. That dress is an odd color.

D. The shirt and tie don't match.

E. Is there a laundromat nearby?

F. I need to do some laundry.

CROSSWORD PUZZLE

Solve the word definitions, then fill in the numbered blanks in the grid.
Answers on page 147.

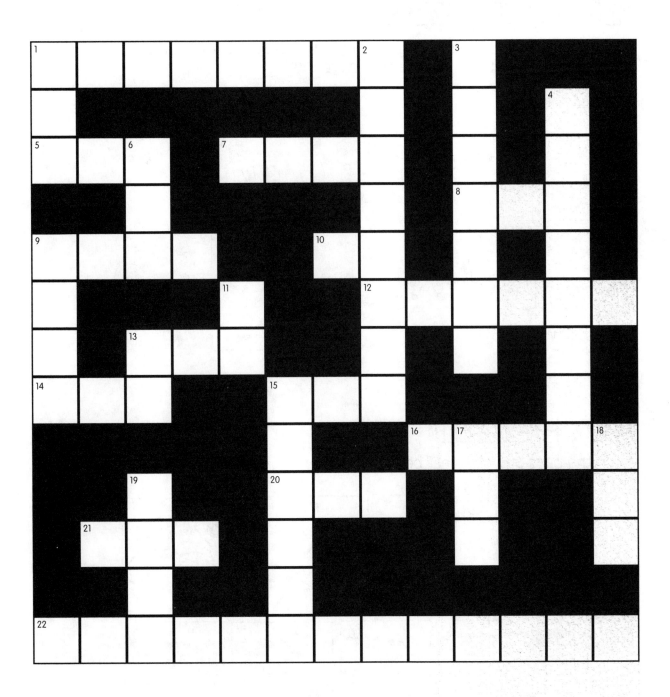

12 SPORTS and RECREATION

ALPHABET PUZZLE

To solve the puzzle, either fill in the blanks with the correct definition or decode the Manual Alphabet key. *Answers on page 148.*

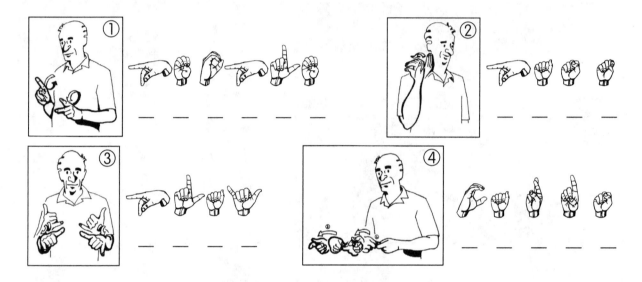

MATCH PUZZLE

Match the pairs of words that belong together.

Answers on page 148.

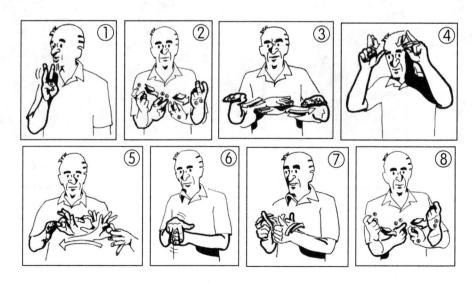

SCRAMBLE PUZZLE

To solve the puzzle, either fill in the blanks with the correct definition or decode the Manual Alphabet key, then unscramble the letters to spell the correct definition.
Answers on page 148.

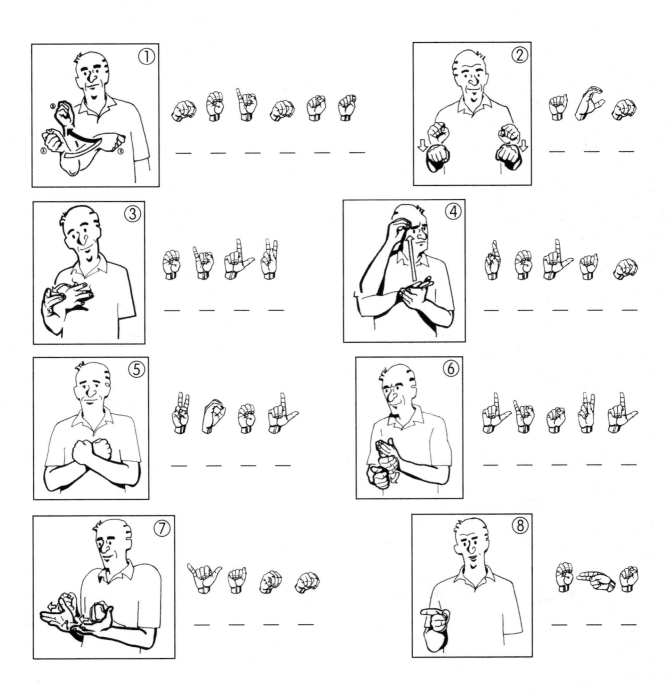

DEFINITION PUZZLE

To solve the puzzle, pick the correct word definition. **Answers on page 148.**

① A. Spring

B. Summer

C. Autumn

② A. Chess

B. Checkers

C. Dominoes

③ A. Chess

B. Checkers

C. Dominoes

④ A. Sailboat

B. Canoe

C. Kayak

⑤ A. Summer

B. Winter

C. Spring

⑥ A. Daily

B. Weekly

C. Monthly

⑦ A. Hiking

B. Hunting

C. Hockey

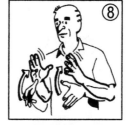

⑧ A. Basketball

B. Football

C. Volleyball

⑨ A. Electronic games

B. Board games

C. Field games

⑩ A. Strong

B. Muscular

C. Exercise

PYRAMID PUZZLE

Solve the word definitions, then fill in the blanks in the pyramid. The signs are grouped in no particular order and the words do not add up to make a sentence. **Answers on page 149.**

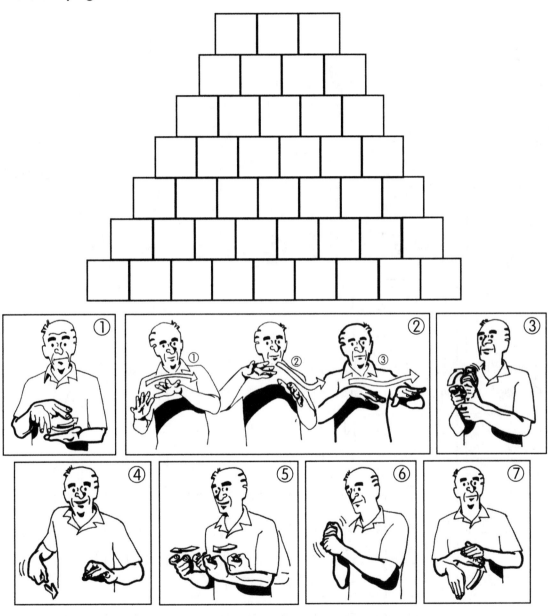

SEARCH PUZZLE

To complete the puzzle, solve the word definitions, then search for words in the grid. Definitions are spelled out vertically, horizontally, diagonally, forward, or backward. **Answers on page 149.**

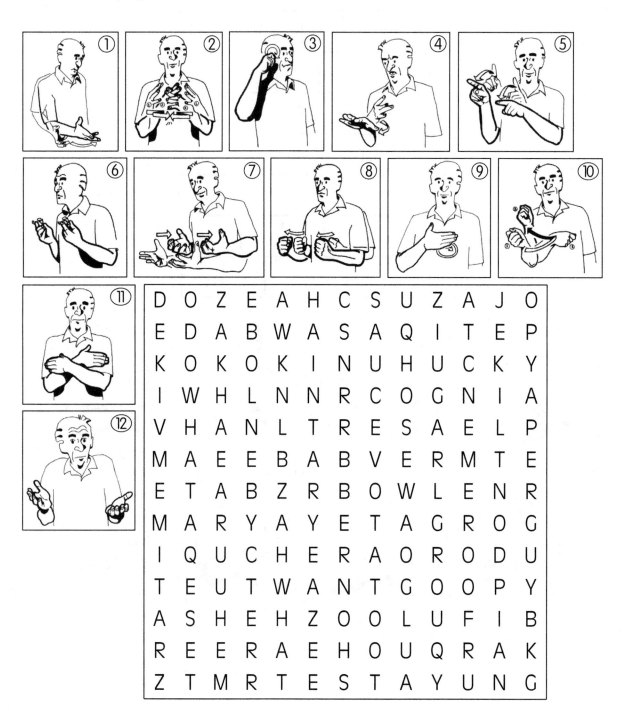

```
D  O  Z  E  A  H  C  S  U  Z  A  J  O
E  D  A  B  W  A  S  A  Q  I  T  E  P
K  O  K  O  K  I  N  U  H  U  C  K  Y
I  W  H  L  N  N  R  C  O  G  N  I  A
V  H  A  N  L  T  R  E  S  A  E  L  P
M  A  E  E  B  A  B  V  E  R  M  T  E
E  T  A  B  Z  R  B  O  W  L  E  N  R
M  A  R  Y  A  Y  E  T  A  G  R  O  G
I  Q  U  C  H  E  R  A  O  R  O  D  U
T  E  U  T  W  A  N  T  G  O  O  P  Y
A  S  H  E  H  Z  O  O  L  U  F  I  B
R  E  E  R  A  E  H  O  U  Q  R  A  K
Z  T  M  R  T  E  S  T  A  Y  U  N  G
```

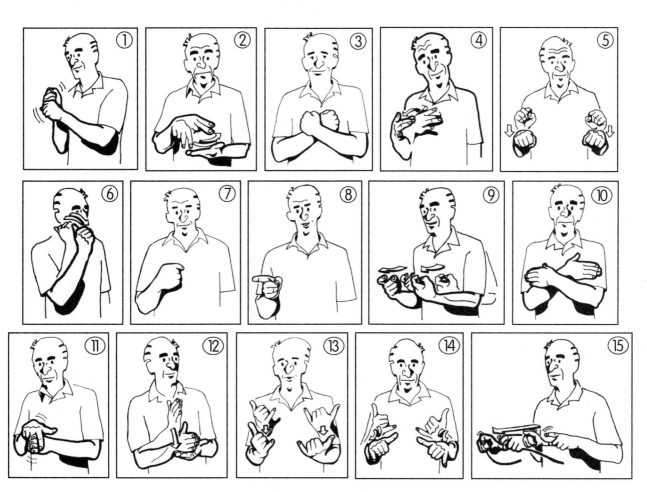

PHRASE PUZZLE

Choose words from the vocabulary list, then put them in the correct order to form the ASL phrases below. **Answers on page 149.**

PHRASES

A. Can you ski?

B. Do you like to play baseball?

C. Let's stop and rest now.

D. She loves to ride horses.

E. I run every day.

F. Do you like to dance?

CROSSWORD PUZZLE

Solve the word definitions, then fill in the numbered blanks in the grid.
Answers on page 149.

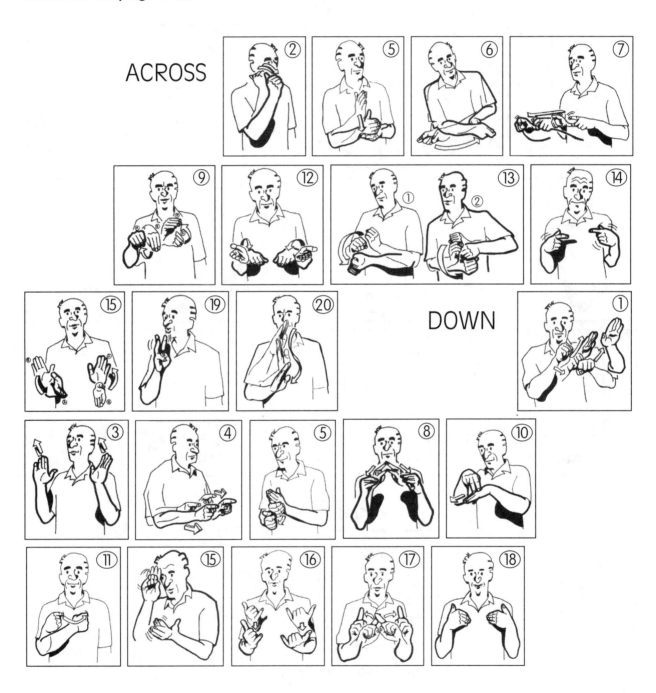

13 — TRAVEL

ALPHABET PUZZLE

To solve the puzzle, either fill in the blanks with the correct definition or decode the Manual Alphabet key. *Answers on page 150.*

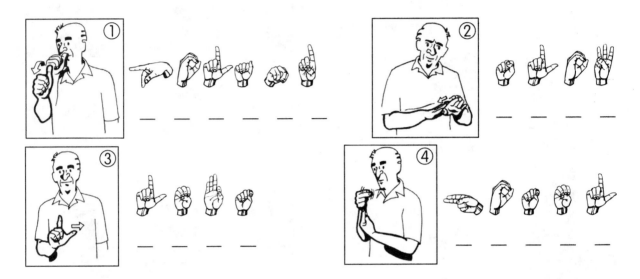

MATCH PUZZLE

Match the pairs of words that belong together.   *Answers on page 150.*

SCRAMBLE PUZZLE

To solve the puzzle, either fill in the blanks with the correct definition or decode the Manual Alphabet key, then unscramble the letters to spell the correct definition.
Answers on page 150.

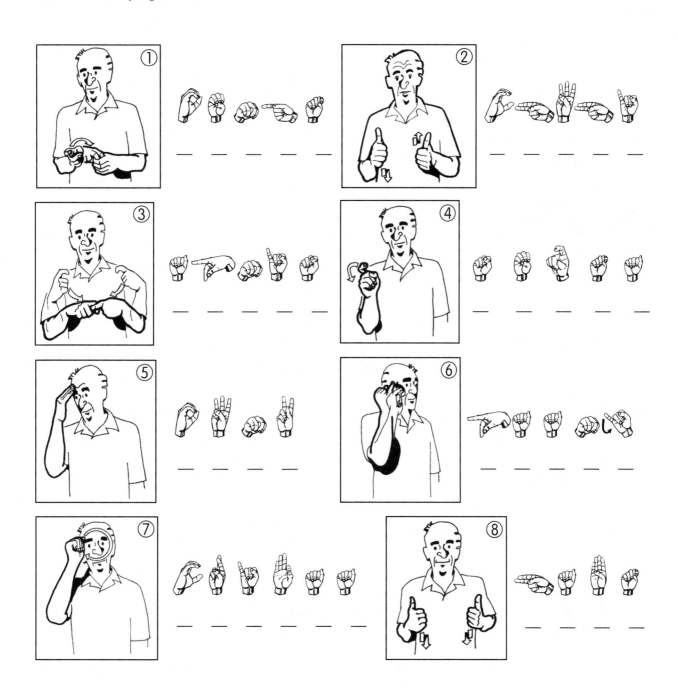

DEFINITION PUZZLE

To solve the puzzle, pick the correct word definition. ***Answers on page 150.***

 ①

A. Car

B. Train

C. Airplane

 ②

A. Airplane take-off

B. Airplane flight

C. Airplane landing

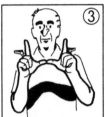 ③

A. License

B. Ticket

C. Passport

④

A. Canada

B. United States

C. Mexico

⑤

A. Ireland

B. Israel

C. Italy

 ⑥

A. Denmark

B. Sweden

C. Norway

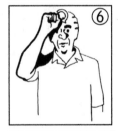 ⑦

A. Washington

B. New York

C. Chicago

 ⑧

A. Airplane take-off

B. Airplane flight

C. Airplane landing

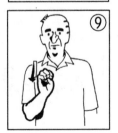 ⑨

A. Elevator

B. Escalator

C. Stairwell

 ⑩

A. Hungary

B. Hawaii

C. Holland

PYRAMID PUZZLE

Solve the word definitions, then fill in the blanks in the pyramid. The signs are grouped in no particular order and the words do not add up to make a sentence.
Answers on page 151.

SEARCH PUZZLE

To complete the puzzle, solve the word definitions, then search for words in the grid. Definitions are spelled out vertically, horizontally, diagonally, forward, or backward. **Answers on page 151.**

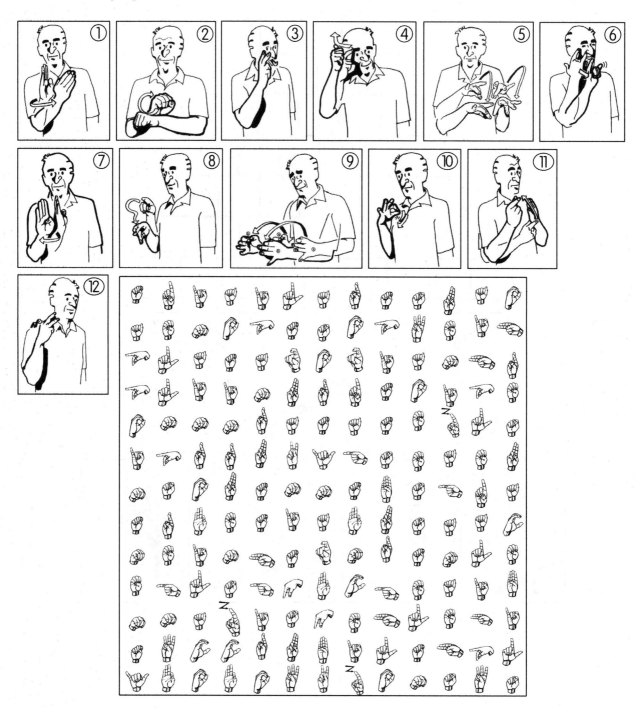

PHRASE PUZZLE

Choose words from the vocabulary list, then put them in the correct order to form the ASL phrases below. ***Answers on page 151.***

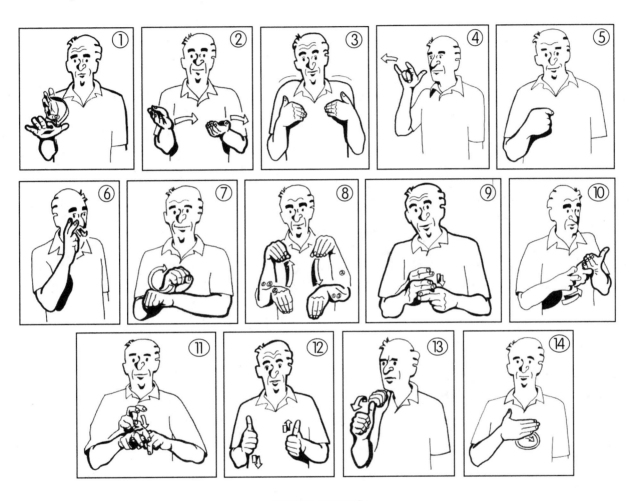

PHRASES

A. Are your bags packed?

B. I'll take you to the airport.

C. Which airline are you taking?

D. The seats are not reserved.

E. May I see your ticket, please?

F. Do you have your ticket?

CROSSWORD PUZZLE

Solve the word definitions, then fill in the numbered blanks in the grid.
Answers on page 151.

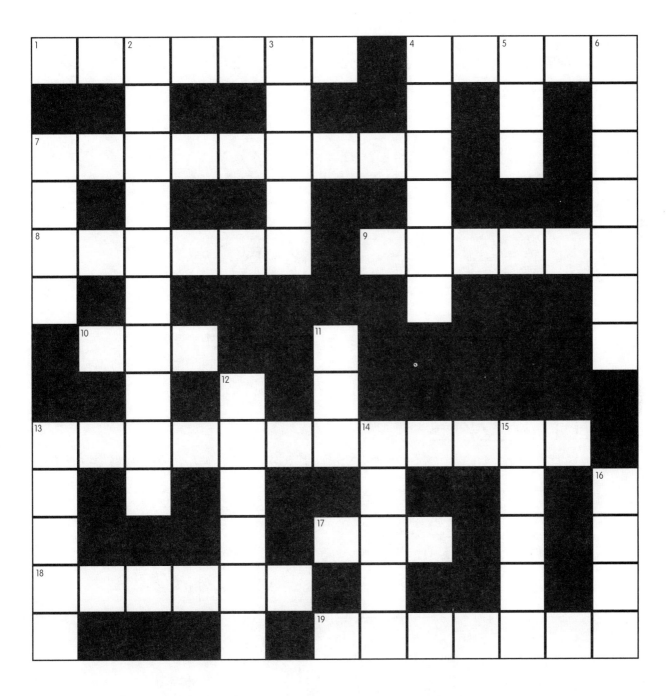

14 ANIMALS and COLORS

ALPHABET PUZZLE

To solve the puzzle, either fill in the blanks with the correct definition or decode the Manual Alphabet key. *Answers on page 152.*

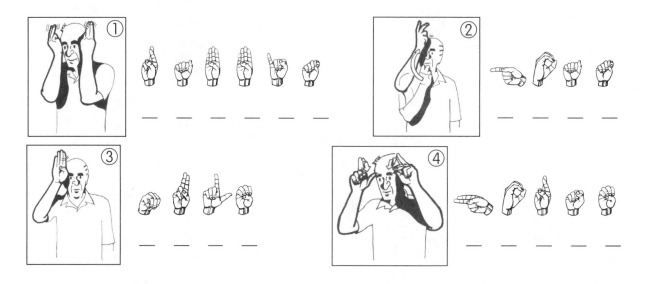

MATCH PUZZLE

Match the pairs of words that belong together.

Answers on page 152.

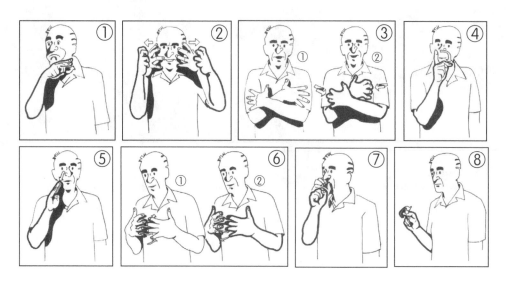

SCRAMBLE PUZZLE

To solve the puzzle, either fill in the blanks with the correct definition or decode the Manual Alphabet key, then unscramble the letters to spell the correct definition.
Answers on page 152.

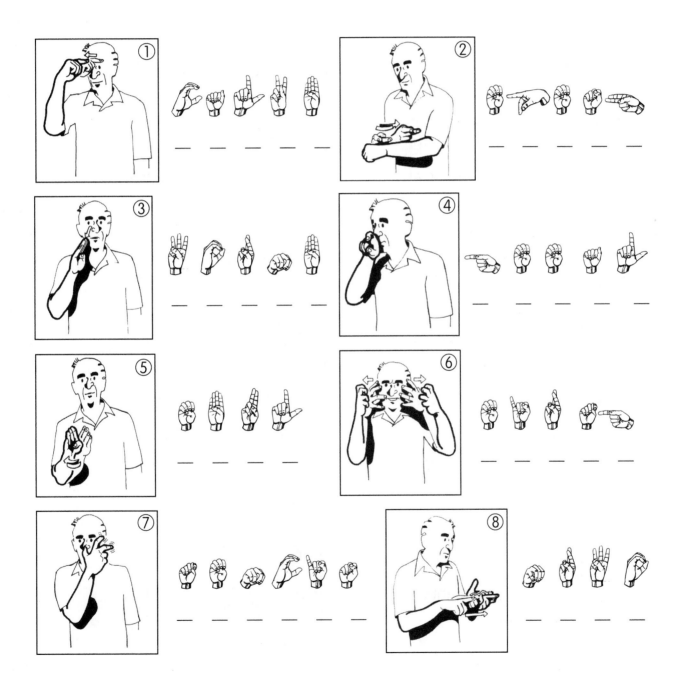

DEFINITION PUZZLE

To solve the puzzle, pick the correct word definition. ***Answers on page 152.***

① A. Lion
B. Tiger
C. Cat

② A. Clear
B. Dark
C. Hazy

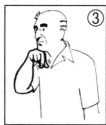
③ A. Rooster
B. Turkey
C. Chicken

④ A. Gorilla
B. Monkey
C. Orangutan

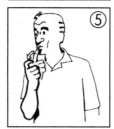
⑤ A. Pink
B. Red
C. Purple

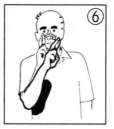
⑥ A. Mouse
B. Rat
C. Raccoon

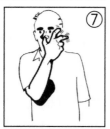
⑦ A. Insect
B. Spider
C. Cockroach

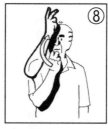
⑧ A. Sheep
B. Bull
C. Goat

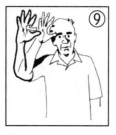
⑨ A. Moose
B. Deer
C. Caribou

⑩ A. Bird
B. Hawk
C. Chicken

PYRAMID PUZZLE

Solve the word definitions, then fill in the blanks in the pyramid. The signs are grouped in no particular order and the words do not add up to make a sentence.
Answers on page 153.

CROSSWORD PUZZLE

Solve the word definitions, then fill in the numbered blanks in the grid.
Answers on page 153.

SEARCH PUZZLE

To complete the puzzle, solve the word definitions, then search for words in the grid. Definitions are spelled out vertically, horizontally, diagonally, forward, or backward.
Answers on page 153.

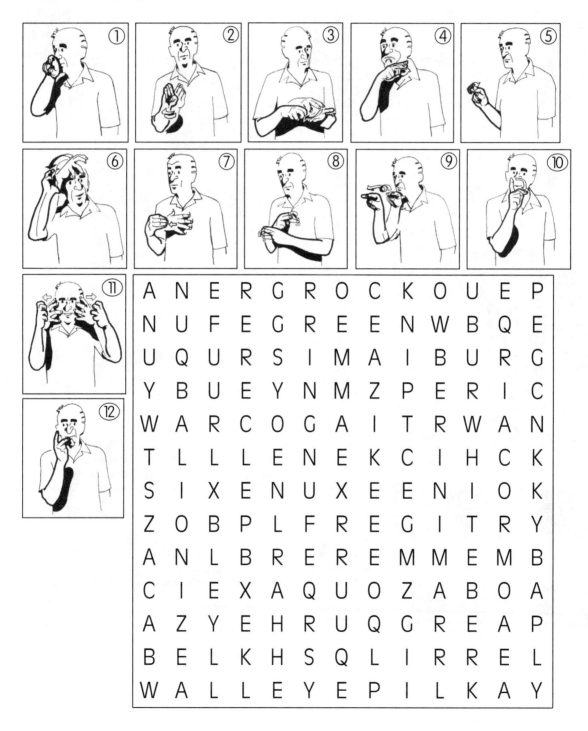

CIVICS

ALPHABET PUZZLE

To solve the puzzle, either fill in the blanks with the correct definition or decode the Manual Alphabet key. *Answers on page 154.*

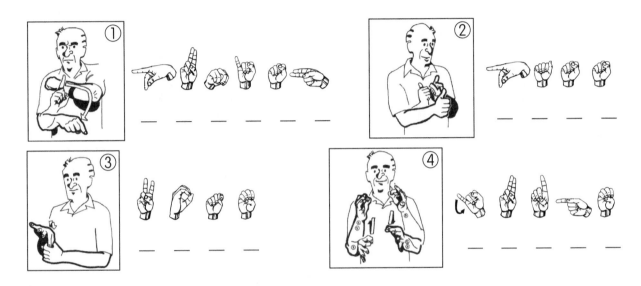

MATCH PUZZLE

Match the pairs of words that belong together.

Answers on page 154.

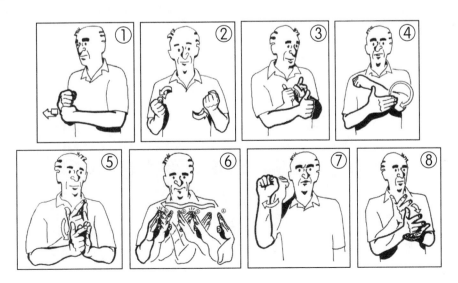

SCRAMBLE PUZZLE

To solve the puzzle, either fill in the blanks with the correct definition or decode the Manual Alphabet key, then unscramble the letters to spell the correct definition.
Answers on page 154.

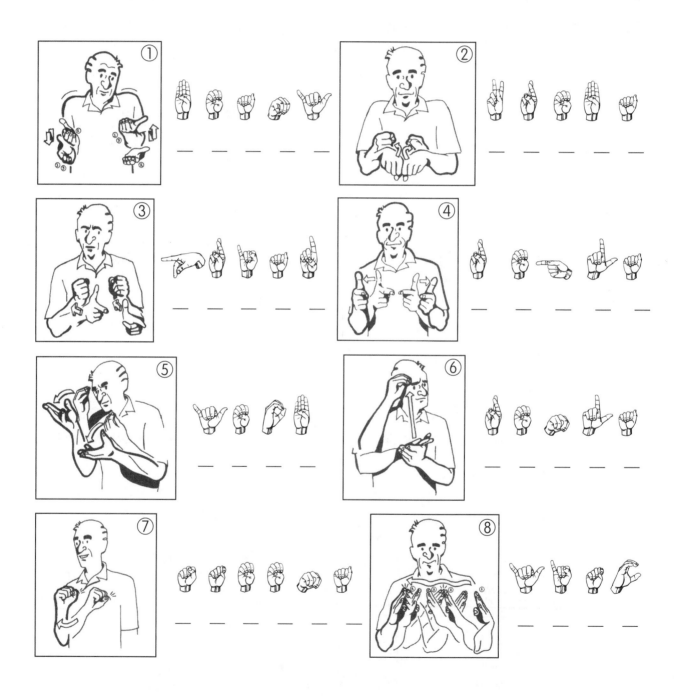

DEFINITION PUZZLE

To solve the puzzle, pick the correct word definition. ***Answers on page 154.***

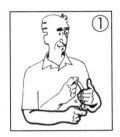 ①

A. Cost

B. Lost

C. Crossed

 ②

A. Too little

B. Too much

C. Too late

 ③

A. This year

B. Next year

C. Last year

 ④

A. Name

B. Same

C. Fame

 ⑤

A. Let

B. Get

C. Met

 ⑥

A. Petition

B. Protest

C. Punish

⑦

A. Disbelieve

B. Discount

C. Disobey

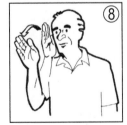 ⑧

A. Will

B. Skill

C. Until

 ⑨

A. All morning

B. All afternoon

C. All night

 ⑩

A. Veto

B. Vote

C. Vex

PYRAMID PUZZLE

Solve the word definitions, then fill in the blanks in the pyramid. The signs are grouped in no particular order and the words do not add up to make a sentence. **Answers on page 155.**

SEARCH PUZZLE

To complete the puzzle, solve the word definitions, then search for words in the grid. Definitions are spelled out vertically, horizontally, diagonally, forward, or backward. **Answers on page 155.**

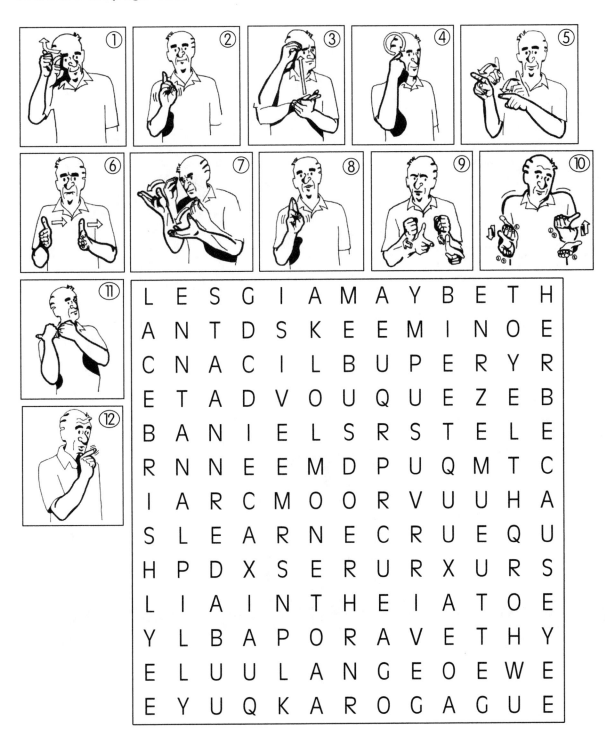

```
L E S G I A M A Y B E T H
A N T D S K E E M I N O E
C N A C I L B U P E R Y R
E T A D V O U Q U E Z E B
B A N I E L S R S T E L E
R N N E E M D P U Q M T C
I A R C M O O R V U U H A
S L E A R N E C R U E Q U
H P D X S E R U R X U R S
L I A I N T H E I A T O E
Y L B A P O R A V E T H Y
E L U U L A N G E O E W E
E Y U Q K A R O G A G U E
```

The American Sign Language Puzzle Book

CROSSWORD PUZZLE

Solve the word definitions, then fill in the numbered blanks in the grid.
Answers on page 155.

ACROSS

DOWN

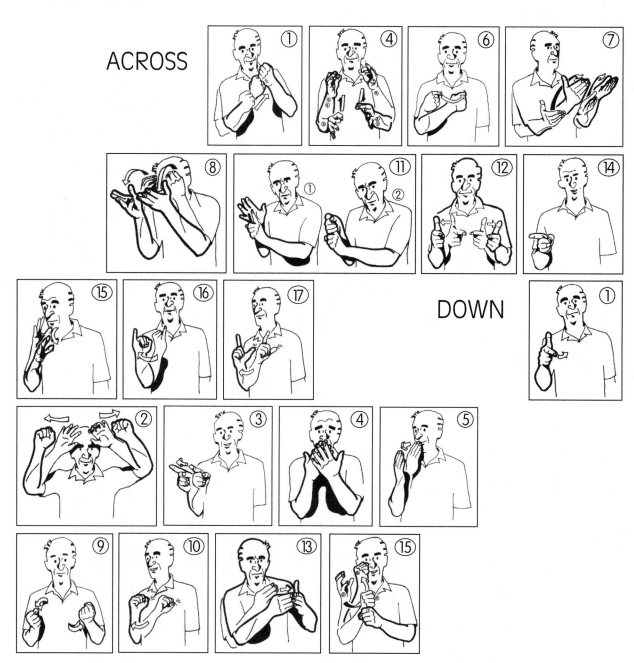

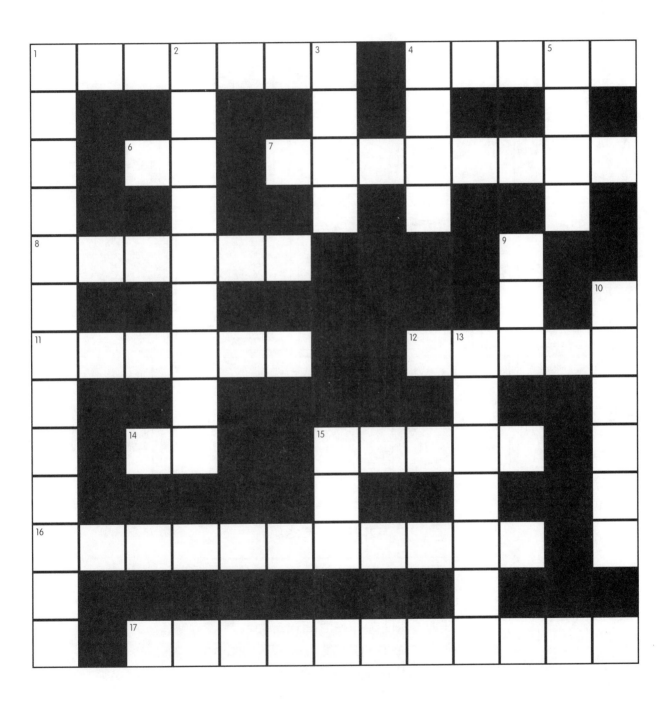

PHRASE PUZZLE

Choose words from the vocabulary list, then put them in the correct order to form the ASL phrases below. *Answers on page 155.*

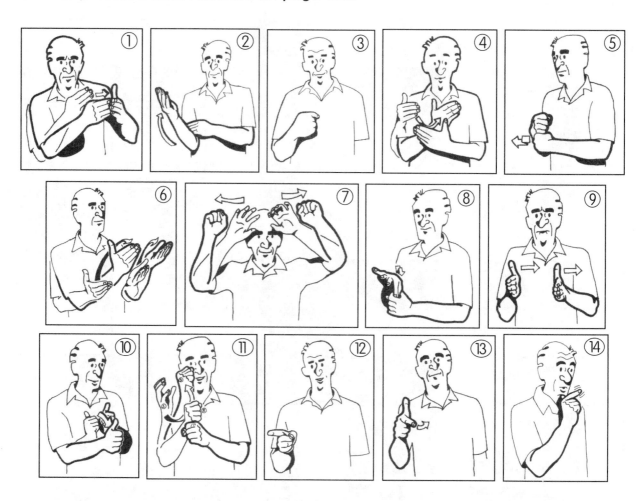

PHRASES

A. I move we pass it.

B. Who won the election?

C. She plans to sue them.

D. I was on the picket line all morning.

E. Who's the new president?

F. I second the motion.

16 RELIGION

ALPHABET PUZZLE

To solve the puzzle, either fill in the blanks with the correct definition or decode the Manual Alphabet key. *Answers on page 156.*

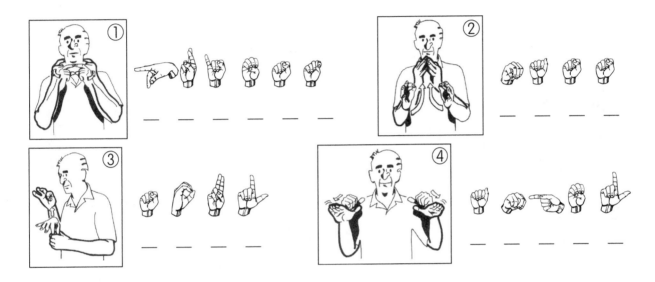

MATCH PUZZLE

Match the pairs of words that belong together.

Answers on page 156.

SCRAMBLE PUZZLE

To solve the puzzle, either fill in the blanks with the correct definition or decode the Manual Alphabet key, then unscramble the letters to spell the correct definition.
Answers on page 156.

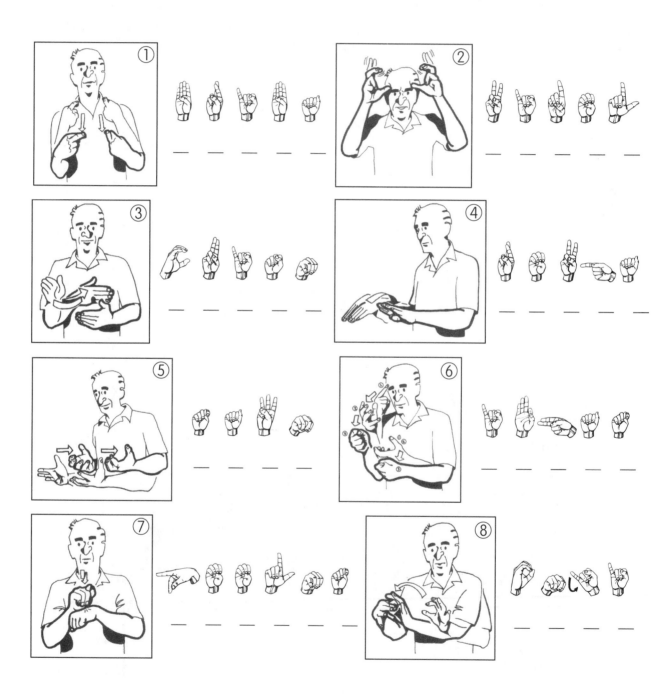

DEFINITION PUZZLE

To solve the puzzle, pick the correct word definition. *Answers on page 156.*

A. Agony

B. Against

C. Again

A. Music

B. Minister

C. Mormon

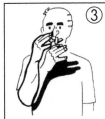

A. Communion

B. Confession

C. Congregation

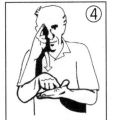

A. Annoint

B. Bless

C. Worship

A. Grave

B. Tombstone

C. Funeral

A. Friday

B. Saturday

C. Sunday

A. Cherish

B. Church

C. Choir

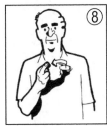

A. Religion

B. Resurrection

C. Rector

A. Heaven

B. Hell

C. Harp

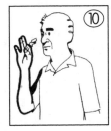

A. Teach

B. Reach

C. Preach

PYRAMID PUZZLE

Solve the word definitions, then fill in the blanks in the pyramid. The signs are grouped in no particular order and the words do not add up to make a sentence. *Answers on page 157.*

SEARCH PUZZLE

To complete the puzzle, solve the word definitions, then search for words in the grid. Definitions are spelled out vertically, horizontally, diagonally, forward, or backward.
Answers on page 157.

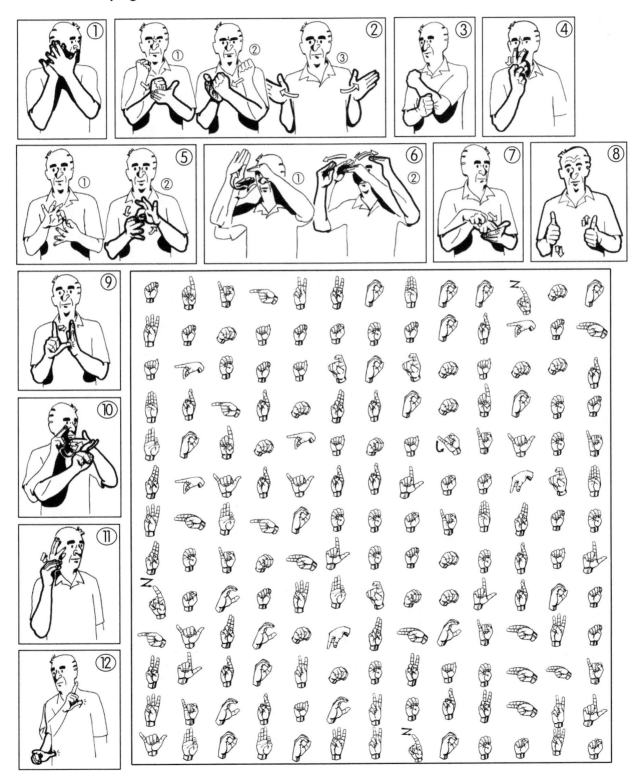

CROSSWORD PUZZLE

Solve the word definitions, then fill in the numbered blanks in the grid.
Answers on page 157.

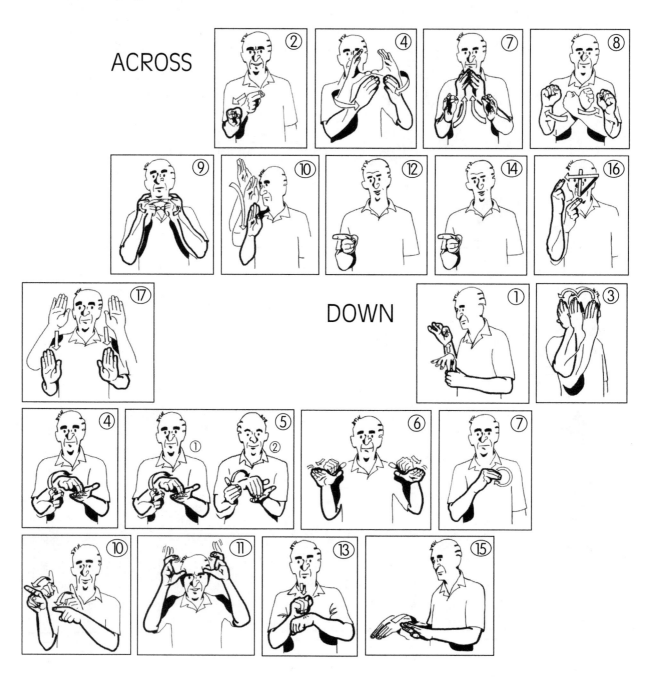

PHRASE PUZZLE

Choose words from the vocabulary list, then put them in the correct order to form the ASL phrases below. *Answers on page 157.*

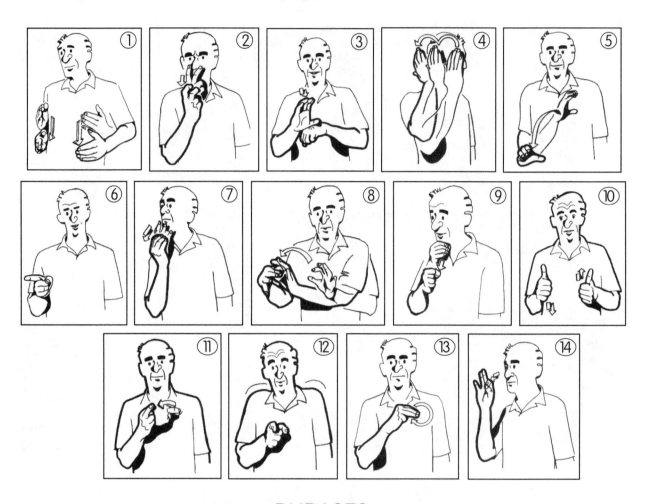

PHRASES

A. He's an atheist.

B. Are you a Christian?

C. He used to be a preacher.

D. Judiasm is an old religion.

E. Which church do you belong to?

F. She's a missionary.

17 NUMBERS, TIME, DATES, and MONEY

ALPHABET PUZZLE

To solve the puzzle, either fill in the blanks with the correct definition or decode the Manual Alphabet key. *Answers on page 158.*

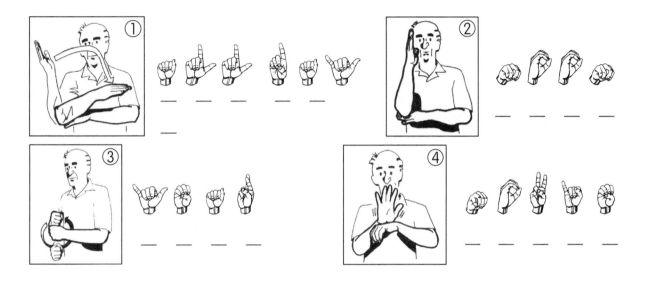

MATCH PUZZLE

Match the pairs of words that belong together.

Answers on page 158.

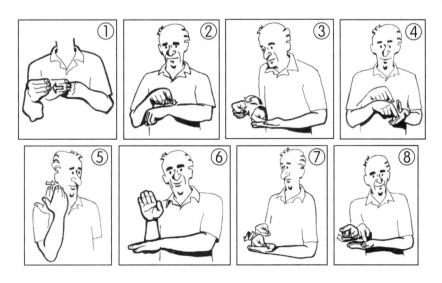

SCRAMBLE PUZZLE

To solve the puzzle, either fill in the blanks with the correct definition or decode the Manual Alphabet key, then unscramble the letters to spell the correct definition.
Answers on page 158.

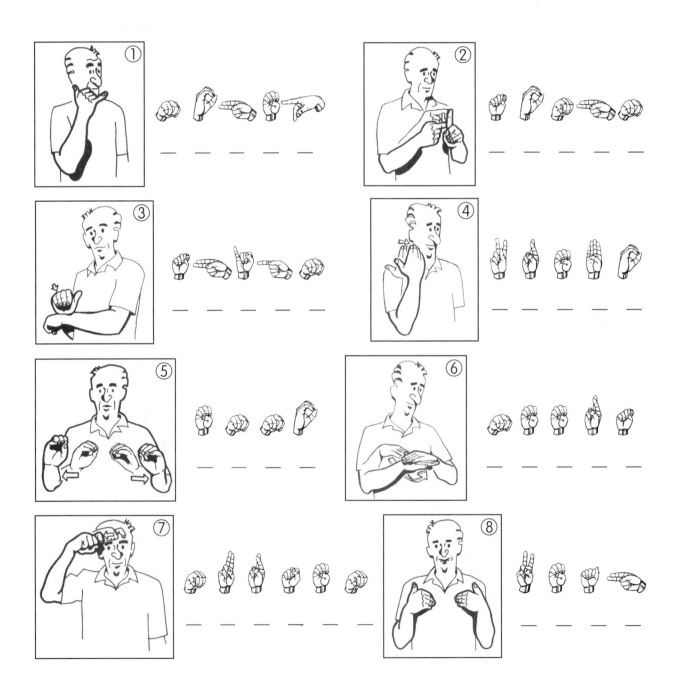

DEFINITION PUZZLE

To solve the puzzle, pick the correct word definition. **Answers on page 158.**

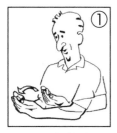 ①

A. Birth

B. Life

C. Death

 ②

A. 10,000

B. 100,000

C. 1,000,000

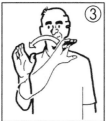 ③

A. Easter

B. Hanukkah

C. Christmas

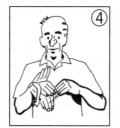 ④

A. Than

B. Then

C. Thin

 ⑤

A. Every Thursday

B. Every Tuesday

C. Every Friday

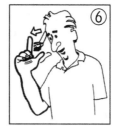 ⑥

A. 10¢

B. 25¢

C. 50¢

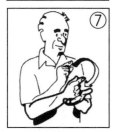 ⑦

A. Graduate

B. College

C. University

 ⑧

A. T-T-Y

B. T-Y-T

C. Y-T-T

 ⑨

A. Summer

B. Autumn

C. Winter

 ⑩

A. Daily

B. Weekly

C. Monthly

PYRAMID PUZZLE

Solve the word definitions, then fill in the blanks in the pyramid. The signs are grouped in no particular order and the words do not add up to make a sentence. *Answers on page 159.*

SEARCH PUZZLE

To complete the puzzle, solve the word definitions, then search for words in the grid.
Definitions are spelled out vertically, horizontally, diagonally, forward, or backward.
Answers on page 159.

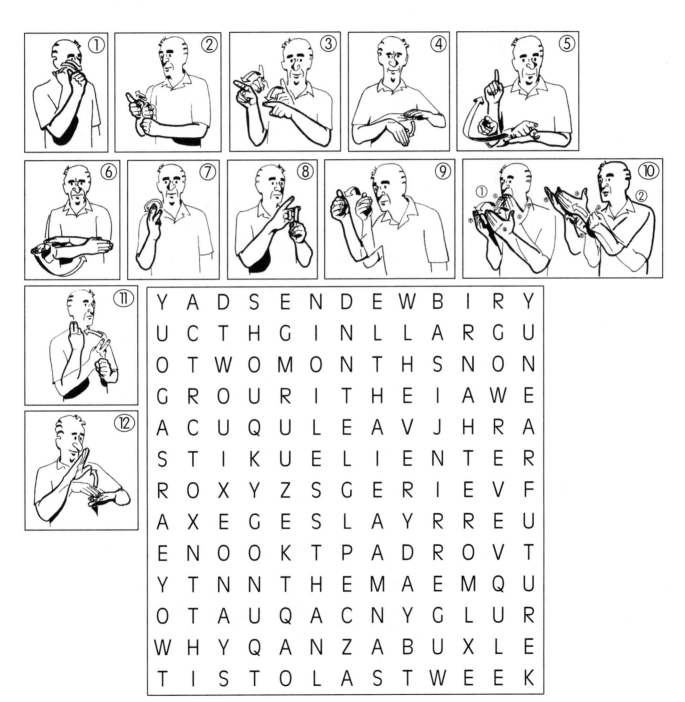

```
Y  A  D  S  E  N  D  E  W  B  I  R  Y
U  C  T  H  G  I  N  L  L  A  R  G  U
O  T  W  O  M  O  N  T  H  S  N  O  N
G  R  O  U  R  I  T  H  E  I  A  W  E
A  C  U  Q  U  L  E  A  V  J  H  R  A
S  T  I  K  U  E  L  I  E  N  T  E  R
R  O  X  Y  Z  S  G  E  R  I  E  V  F
A  X  E  G  E  S  L  A  Y  R  R  E  U
E  N  O  O  K  T  P  A  D  R  O  V  T
Y  T  N  N  T  H  E  M  A  E  M  Q  U
O  T  A  U  Q  A  C  N  Y  G  L  U  R
W  H  Y  Q  A  N  Z  A  B  U  X  L  E
T  I  S  T  O  L  A  S  T  W  E  E  K
```

CROSSWORD PUZZLE

Solve the word definitions, then fill in the numbered blanks in the grid.
Answers on page 159.

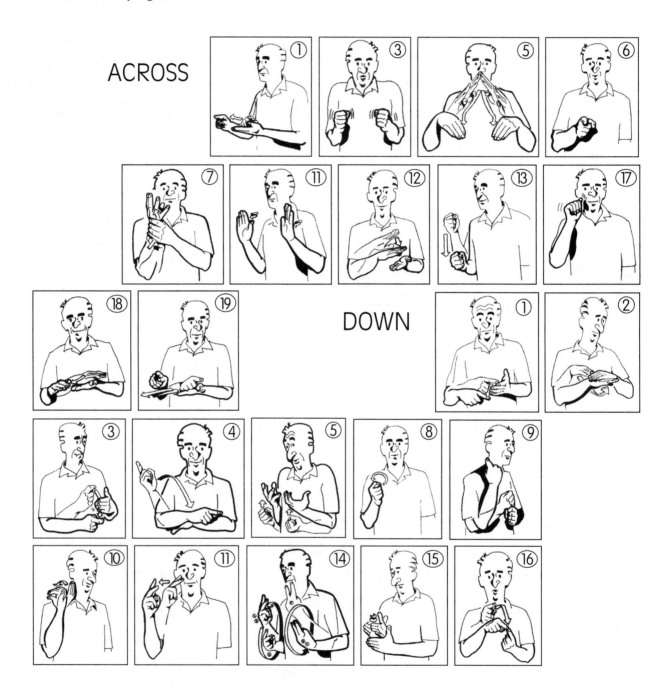

ACROSS

DOWN

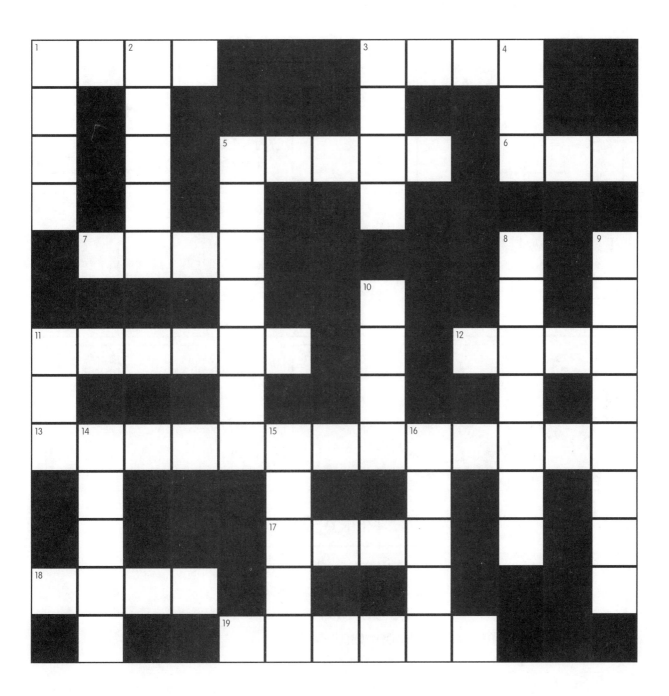

PHRASE PUZZLE

Choose words from the vocabulary list, then put them in the correct order to form the ASL phrases below. *Answers on page 159.*

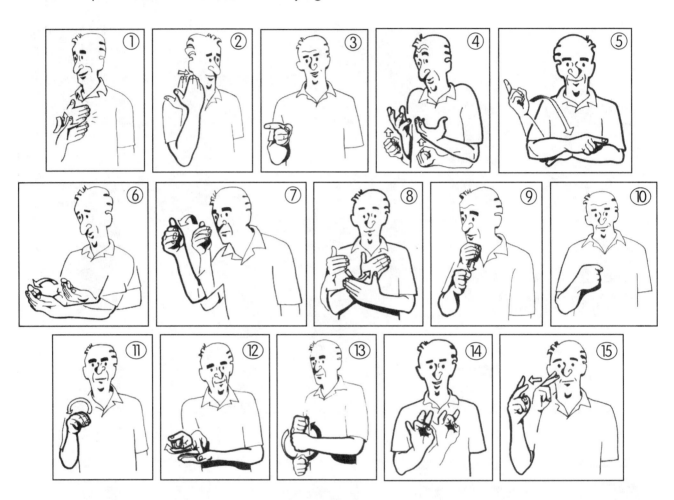

PHRASES

A. How much did you pay?

B. I'll see you next Monday.

C. He is 87 years old.

D. Happy birthday.

E. Happy New Year.

F. I'm broke.

ANSWER KEY

CHAPTER 3

ALPHABET PUZZLE *page 10*

① P L E A S E

② H A V E

③ L O O K

④ S O R R Y

DEFINITION PUZZLE *page 12*

① A. To
B. For
C. With

② A. Sooner
B. Later
C. Now

③ A. A lot
B. Some
C. None

④ **A. Number**
B. Letter
C. Symbol

⑤ **A. Fine**
B. Mine
C. Combine

⑥ A. Know
B. Think
C. Feel

⑦ A. Tried
B. Tiered
C. Tired

⑧ A. Truck
B. Car
C. Bus

⑨ **A. Sick**
B. Trick
C. Thick

⑩ A. Health
B. Head
C. Home

MATCH PUZZLE *page 10*

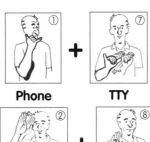 +
Phone   **TTY**

 +
Hello   **Good-bye**

 +
Good   **Lousy**

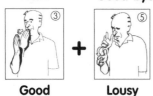 +
Open door   **Open window**

SCRAMBLE PUZZLE *page 11*

①  O N G G I
(GOING)

②  L O H E L
(HELLO)

③ I D E R T
(TIRED)

④ H E W E R
(WHERE)

⑤ I C S K
(SICK)

⑥ U L Y O S
(LOUSY)

⑦ S C E E U X
(EXCUSE)

⑧ E I M T
(TIME)

130

SEARCH PUZZLE *page 14*

```
Z A K U X E T O R Y L E J
A W U Z Y J W L U M O Z O
H G A D B O W I P E Q U K
Y E L N O N H K T K I D O
E P O Y T J E E I E R M U
F I P S W I R R L P O P Q
W O U A F T E R N O O N U
U M R R H E B K O N D I R
X I K O B Z Y L W D E X L
O J R T T I R R A Y S E K
Z L A L U F R E D N O W E
A H R W N I X N Y E L O Y
W O D N I W E S O L C N E
```

1. AFTERNOON
2. CLOSE DOOR
3. WHERE
4. HAPPY
5. LIKE
6. MUST
7. CLOSE WINDOW
8. WHAT
9. WANT
10. UP TIL NOW
11. WONDERFUL

CROSSWORD PUZZLE *page 16*

PYRAMID PUZZLE *page 13*

```
        T V
       S I T
      L O N G
     N I G H T
    E X C U S E
   G O O D B Y E
  A L L R I G H T
```

Night   Excuse   Sit
All right   T.V.   Long   Good-bye

PHRASE PUZZLE *page 15*

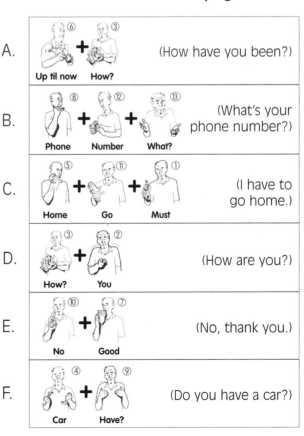

A. Up til now + How? (How have you been?)
B. Phone + Number + What? (What's your phone number?)
C. Home + Go + Must (I have to go home.)
D. How? + You (How are you?)
E. No + Good (No, thank you.)
F. Car + Have? (Do you have a car?)

131

CHAPTER 4

ALPHABET PUZZLE *page 18*

  ①
P L E A S E

  ②
M E A N

  ③
M A N Y

  ④
V I S I T

DEFINITION PUZZLE *page 20*

①
A. Bit
B. Bet
C. But

②
A. Choose
B. Lose
C. Shoes

③
A. Word
B. Sentence
C. Language

④
A. Past
B. Pest
C. Post

⑤
A. For
B. Form
C. Fortune

⑥
A. Wait
B. Want
C. Went

⑦
A. Day
B. Noon
C. Night

⑧
A. Underdone
B. Understand
C. Underfoot

⑨
A. Got
B. Hot
C. Not

⑩
A. Mother
B. Father
C. Parent

MATCH PUZZLE *page 18*

① **Deaf**   +   ⑦ **Sign**

② **Blind**   +   ⑧ **Braille**

③ **School**   +   ⑤ **Learn**

④ **Movie**   +   ⑥  **T.V.**

SCRAMBLE PUZZLE *page 19*

①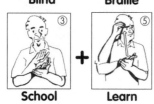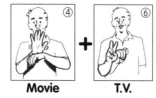
M E E C B O
(BECOME)

②
O F R
(FOR)

③
O G D O
(GOOD)

④
A K S E P
(SPEAK)

⑤
T H W A
(WHAT)

⑥
I R P A D
(RAPID)

⑦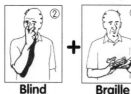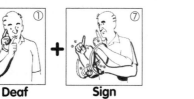
E N N O
(NONE)

⑧
E F D A
(DEAF)

SEARCH PUZZLE *page 22*

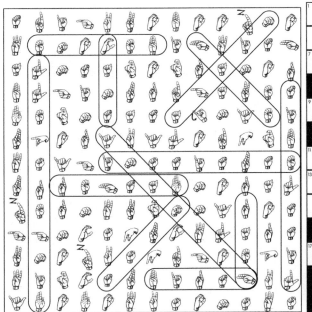

1. FATHER
2. BIRTH
3. LITTLE BIT
4. AGAIN
5. HAVE
6. CAN'T
7. INSTITUTE
8. FINGERSPELL
9. HEAR
10. HOW MANY
11. BECOME
12. MUST

CROSSWORD PUZZLE *page 24*

PYRAMID PUZZLE *page 21*

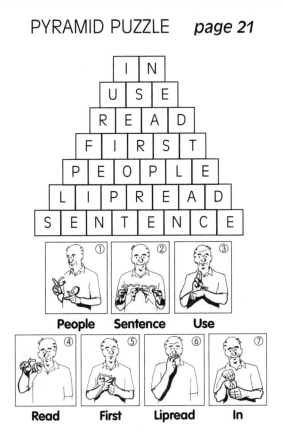

People Sentence Use

Read First Lipread In

PHRASE PUZZLE *page 23*

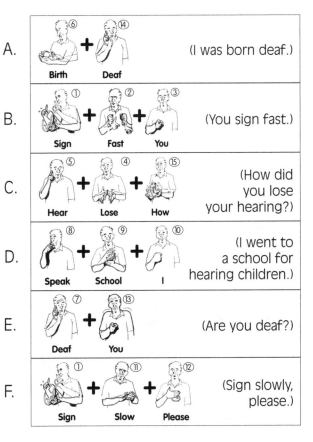

A. Birth + Deaf (I was born deaf.)

B. Sign + Fast + You (You sign fast.)

C. Hear + Lose + How (How did you lose your hearing?)

D. Speak + School + I (I went to a school for hearing children.)

E. Deaf + You (Are you deaf?)

F. Sign + Slow + Please (Sign slowly, please.)

Answer Key

CHAPTER 5

ALPHABET PUZZLE *page 26*

S C H O O L

W I F E

L I V E

P O L I C E

DEFINITION PUZZLE *page 28*

 ①
A. Friend
B. Fend
C. Fired

 ②
A. Bold
B. Cold
C. Old

 ③
A. Reach
B. Each
C. Teach

 ④
A. Name
B. Game
C. Same

 ⑤
A. Policeman
B. Firefighter
C. Soldier

⑥
A. Aft
B. Art
C. Act

⑦
A. Have
B. Heave
C. Heavy

⑧
A. Law
B. Low
C. Allow

⑨
A. Interfere
B. Introduce
C. Interpret

 ⑩
A. Parent
B. Daughter
C. Son

MATCH PUZZLE *page 26*

① Cigarette + ⑧ Match

② Marry + ⑦ Divorced

③ Husband + ⑤ Wife

④ Work + ⑥ Secretary

SCRAMBLE PUZZLE *page 27*

①  O R J M A (MAJOR)

②  S H E O U (HOUSE)

③ T R I B H (BIRTH)

④ P H Y P A (HAPPY)

⑤  K O R W (WORK)

⑥ 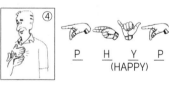 T H A M C (MATCH)

⑦ 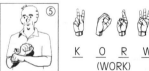 R O O T C D (DOCTOR)

⑧  N Y L O (ONLY)

134

SEARCH PUZZLE   *page 30*

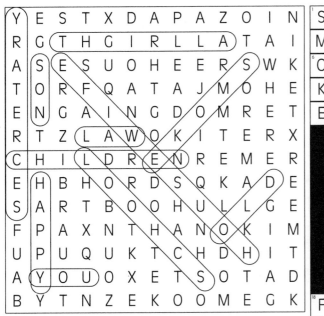

1. HAPPY
2. YOU
3. OLD
4. LAW
5. SCHOOL
6. CHILDREN
7. SECRETARY
8. HOUSEWIFE
9. ALL RIGHT
10. SMOKE
11. SON

CROSSWORD PUZZLE   *page 32*

PYRAMID PUZZLE   *page 29*

PHRASE PUZZLE   *page 31*

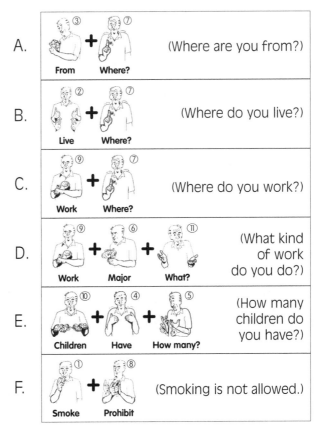

A. From + Where?   (Where are you from?)

B. Live + Where?   (Where do you live?)

C. Work + Where?   (Where do you work?)

D. Work + Major + What?   (What kind of work do you do?)

E. Children + Have + How many?   (How many children do you have?)

F. Smoke + Prohibit   (Smoking is not allowed.)

CHAPTER 6

ALPHABET PUZZLE *page 34*

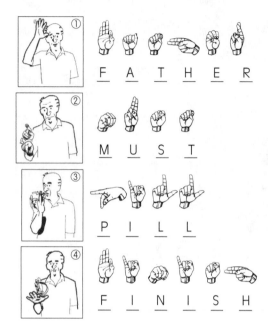

① F A T H E R

② M U S T

③ P I L L

④ F I N I S H

DEFINITION PUZZLE *page 36*

① A. Which?
B. Why?
C. Where?

② A. All over
B. All right
C. All ready

③ A. Born
B. Die
C. Live

④ A. Bath
B. Both
C. Berth

⑤ A. Gold
B. Glad
C. Good

⑥ A. Beckon
B. Become
C. Before

⑦ A. You
B. Yourself
C. Yourselves

⑧ A. Hair dryer
B. Hair curl
C. Hair rinse

⑨ A. Next week
B. Last week
C. First week

⑩ A. Interrrupt
B. Independent
C. Insurance

MATCH PUZZLE *page 34*

① Dentist + ⑥ Pull tooth

② Shower + ⑧ Wash face

③ Headache + ⑤ Medicine

④ Hospital + ⑦ Emergency vehicle

SCRAMBLE PUZZLE *page 35*

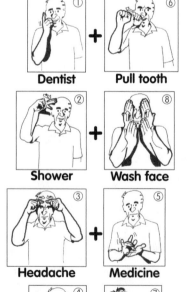
① A C R E S H
(SEARCH)

② Y A N
(ANY)

③ V E H A
(HAVE)

④ E K B R A
(BREAK)

⑤ C M U H
(MUCH)

⑥ H E S V A
(SHAVE)

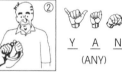

⑦ M E I T
(TIME)

⑧ E B D
(BED)

SEARCH PUZZLE   *page 38*

E	X	T	B	W	O	U	S	E	D	U	P	O
H	T	S	U	G	S	I	D	L	E	T	Q	U
S	O	S	D	N	A	H	H	S	A	W	A	R
U	P	T	I	L	N	O	W	F	C	S	I	D
R	U	R	N	Z	Y	J	O	I	Z	B	E	R
B	I	R	F	X	O	A	M	X	I	R	B	A
H	A	J	H	Y	E	R	C	H	S	U	E	W
T	R	E	T	T	E	B	Y	N	I	S	G	B
O	F	S	O	D	X	O	H	I	N	H	A	L
O	S	T	O	M	A	C	H	A	C	H	E	O
T	Z	P	A	S	H	R	S	P	Y	A	M	O
B	Y	P	N	Q	A	F	H	A	R	I	L	D
H	U	E	S	O	N	Y	N	N	U	R	E	W

1. BETTER	5. UP TIL NOW	9. HYPODERMIC
2. TOOTHBRUSH	6. BRUSH HAIR	10. PAIN
3. DISGUST	7. USED UP	11. RUNNY NOSE
4. DRAW BLOOD	8. WASH HANDS	12. STOMACHACHE

CROSSWORD PUZZLE   *page 40*

A	P	P	O	I	N	T	M	E	N	T		L
	U					Y		O				I
	L	L	O	S	E				W	I	F	E
C	L					L					D	
O	T	O	O	T	H	A	C	H	E		O	W
M	O				T		O				W	N
B	L	O	W	N	O	S	E		W			N
T				F							
	T	H	E	R	M	O	M	E	T	E	R	
	O			E							
H	U	S	B	A	N	D		L	E	N	D	
	U		T					O			
B	O	D	Y	H	O	S	P	I	T	A	L	

PYRAMID PUZZLE   *page 37*

```
          I
        M   Y
      F   O   R
    W   A   N   T
  B   L   O   O   D
D   O   C   T   O   R
S   U   R   G   E   R   Y
```

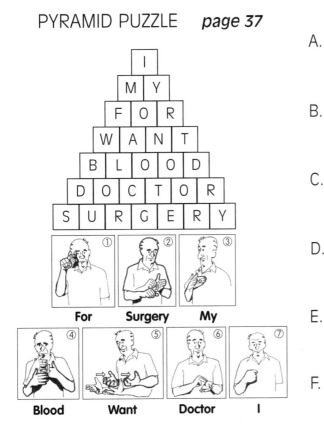

① For   ② Surgery   ③ My
④ Blood   ⑤ Want   ⑥ Doctor   ⑦ I

PHRASE PUZZLE   *page 39*

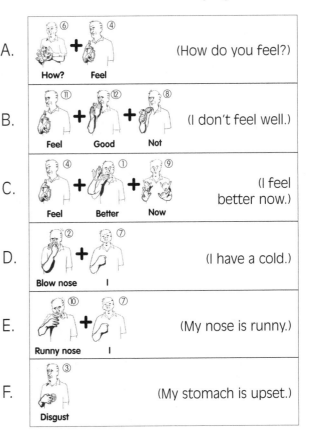

A. ⑥ How? + ④ Feel   (How do you feel?)

B. ⑪ Feel + ⑫ Good + ⑧ Not   (I don't feel well.)

C. ④ Feel + ① Better + ⑨ Now   (I feel better now.)

D. ② Blow nose + ⑦ I   (I have a cold.)

E. ⑩ Runny nose + ⑦ I   (My nose is runny.)

F. ③ Disgust   (My stomach is upset.)

CHAPTER 7

ALPHABET PUZZLE   *page 42*

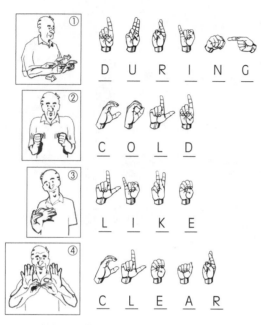

① D U R I N G

② C O L D

③ L I K E

④ C L E A R

DEFINITION PUZZLE   *page 44*

 ①
A. Morning
B. **Afternoon**
C. Night

 ②
A. Show
B. Slow
C. **Grow**

 ③
A. **Sunset**
B. Sunrise
C. Sunday

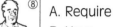 ④
A. Before
B. **During**
C. After

 ⑤
A. **Lightning**
B. Lighting
C. Lighter

 ⑥
A. Launch
B. Ramp
C. **Mountain**

 ⑦
A. Last
B. **Past**
C. Fast

 ⑧
A. **Require**
B. Have
C. Sell

 ⑨
A. Yesterday
B. Today
C. **Tomorrow**

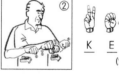 ⑩
A. **Rubber**
B. Runner
C. Rudder

MATCH PUZZLE   *page 42*

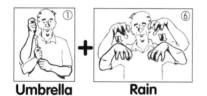
Umbrella + **Rain** ① ⑥

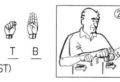
Galoshes + **Flood** ② ⑦

Summer + **Hot** ③ ④

Chain + **Snow** ⑤ ⑧

SCRAMBLE PUZZLE   *page 43*

 ①
S E T B
(BEST)

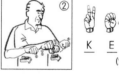 ②
K E H A S
(SHAKE)

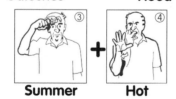 ③
I N A R
(RAIN)

 ④
B Y M E A
(MAYBE)

 ⑤
L M T E
(MELT)

 ⑥
O P E H
(HOPE)

 ⑦
M U R M E S
(SUMMER)

 ⑧
E I C
(ICE)

138

SEARCH PUZZLE   *page 46*

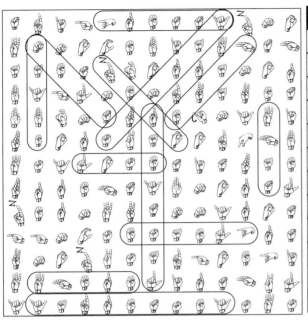

1. HAVE
2. LAST YEAR
3. LOSE
4. MAYBE
5. MELT
6. PLEASE
7. PRETTY
8. ZERO
9. WHERE?
10. WHAT?
11. YESTERDAY
12. SUNRAY

CROSSWORD PUZZLE   *page 48*

PYRAMID PUZZLE   *page 45*

Water   Tornado   Finish

Sun   Less than   Coat

PHRASE PUZZLE   *page 47*

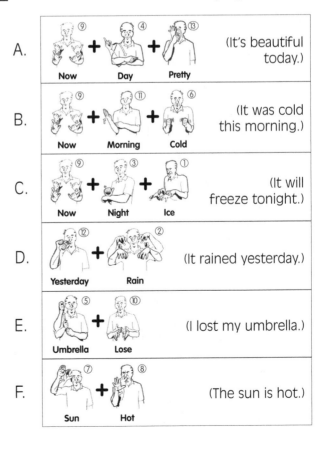

A.   Now + Day + Pretty   (It's beautiful today.)

B.   Now + Morning + Cold   (It was cold this morning.)

C.   Now + Night + Ice   (It will freeze tonight.)

D.   Yesterday + Rain   (It rained yesterday.)

E.   Umbrella + Lose   (I lost my umbrella.)

F.   Sun + Hot   (The sun is hot.)

CHAPTER 8

ALPHABET PUZZLE   *page 50*

① R O C K E T

② F A C E

③ G I R L

④ T A L K

DEFINITION PUZZLE   *page 52*

① A. Took
B. Cook
C. Book

② **A. Break**
B. Shake
C. Make

③ A. Charm
B. Farm
C. Arm

④ **A. Live**
B. Give
C. Sieve

⑤ A. Yell
B. Sell
C. Tell

⑥ **A. Will**
B. Fill
C. Chill

⑦ A. Glove
B. Love
C. Above

⑧ A. You
B. Your
C. Yourself

⑨ A. Slice
B. Twice
C. Nice

⑩ A. Skill
B. Spill
C. Still

MATCH PUZZLE   *page 50*

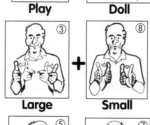
① Airplane + ⑥ Rocket

② Play + ④ Doll

③ Large + ⑧ Small

⑤ Mother + ⑦ Baby

SCRAMBLE PUZZLE   *page 51*

①  T R A F E H (FATHER)

②  O S N (SON)

③ A T H T (THAT)

④ E W E S T (SWEET)

⑤ K W R O (WORK)

⑥ G L E A R (LARGE)

⑦ V O L E (LOVE)

⑧ U Y O (YOU)

SEARCH PUZZLE   *page 54*

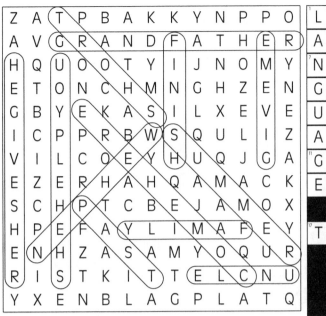

Z A T P B A K K Y N P P O
A V G R A N D F A T H E R
H Q U O O T Y I J N O M Y
E T O N C H M N G H Z E N
G B Y E K A S I L X E V E
I C P P R B W S Q U L I Z
V I L C O E Y H U Q J G A
E Z E R H A H Q A M A C K
S C H P T C B E J A M O X
H P E F A Y L I M A F E Y
E N H Z A S A M Y O Q U R
R I S T K I T T E L C N U
Y X E N B L A G P L A T Q

1. COME HERE
2. GRANDFATHER
3. FINISH
4. NEPHEW
5. GIVE ME
6. UNCLE
7. SHE HELP YOU
8. PAST
9. HE GIVES HER
10. SHORT
11. FAMILY
12. SUMMER

CROSSWORD PUZZLE   *page 56*

				S	I	S	T	E	R			
L			F		E		M			B	O	Y
A		N	I	E	C	E		A	U	N	T	O
N		G		W				L		H		U
G		U		C	H	I	L	D	R	E	N	N
U		A		O					R		G
A		G	R	A	N	D	M	O	T	H	E	R
G		E		V		A		O		O	U	R
E		W	E		N		W		C	
T	H	A	N		E	A	I	M	K	I
O		E			A	G	E	N	T	S
W	O	M	A	N		T	
H	E	R	E		Y		Y	

PYRAMID PUZZLE   *page 53*

		A	S		
	O	U	T		
	C	I	T	Y	
S	W	E	E	T	
C	O	U	S	I	N
B	R	O	T	H	E	R
D	A	U	G	H	T	E	R

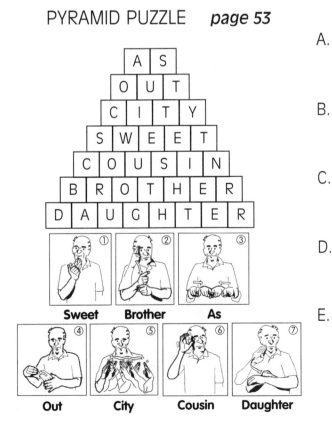

① Sweet ② Brother ③ As
④ Out ⑤ City ⑥ Cousin ⑦ Daughter

PHRASE PUZZLE   *page 55*

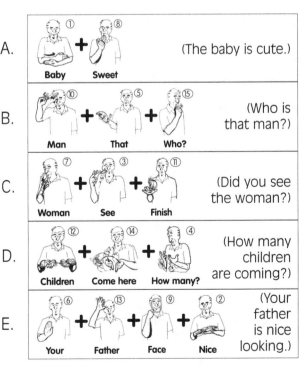

A. ① Baby + ⑧ Sweet (The baby is cute.)

B. ⑩ Man + ⑤ That + ⑮ Who? (Who is that man?)

C. ⑦ Woman + ③ See + ⑪ Finish (Did you see the woman?)

D. ⑫ Children + ⑭ Come here + ④ How many? (How many children are coming?)

E. ⑥ Your + ⑬ Father + ⑨ Face + ② Nice (Your father is nice looking.)

CHAPTER 9

ALPHABET PUZZLE *page 58*

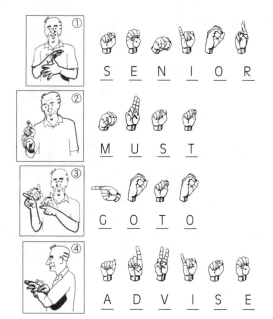

S E N I O R

M U S T

G O T O

A D V I S E

DEFINITION PUZZLE *page 60*

 ① A. All night
B. All day
C. All the time

 ② A. Pen
B. Pencil
C. Paper

 ③ A. Friend
B. Lend
C. Mend

 ④ A. Computer
B. Calculator
C. Typewriter

 ⑤ A. Chemistry
B. History
C. Drama

 ⑥ A. Discuss
B. Dismiss
C. Discover

 ⑦ A. This year
B. Next year
C. Last year

 ⑧ A. Plus
B. Pass
C. Period

⑨ A. Week
B. Year
C. Semester

⑩ A. English
B. French
C. Spanish

MATCH PUZZLE *page 58*

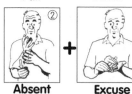 ① Fail +  ④ Flunk

② Absent + ⑦ Excuse

③ Research + ⑤ Study

⑥ College + ⑧ Education

SCRAMBLE PUZZLE *page 59*

① A L N E R (LEARN)

② E K R A B (BREAK)

③ O W W T E (WE TWO)

④ I D B L U (BUILD)

⑤ K A L T (TALK)

⑥ E L E P S (SLEEP)

⑦ N U G R I D (DURING)

⑧ 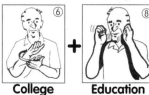 O T N D (DON'T)

SEARCH PUZZLE   *page 62*

W	E	R	A	S	E	B	O	A	R	D	Z	M
A	X	W	O	R	R	O	M	O	T	E	E	T
C	O	R	Y	U	O	Z	A	X	O	Y	A	O
A	T	A	N	A	M	H	S	E	R	F	P	N
L	A	N	R	P	O	L	Y	T	I	E	X	E
C	T	I	B	I	H	O	R	P	N	E	O	Z
U	Y	N	Z	I	P	N	R	B	E	M	O	W
L	P	H	I	L	O	S	O	P	H	Y	T	E
A	A	T	A	H	S	O	T	O	A	R	M	J
T	R	A	N	I	K	O	N	K	R	E	S	T
O	E	G	E	E	L	B	A	S	V	U	V	E
R	H	F	U	U	G	I	T	I	U	Q	U	E
Z	T	U	Q	N	E	A	G	X	E	L	E	P

1. TOMORROW	5. PROHIBIT	9. CALCULATOR
2. THERAPY	6. QUERY ME	10. OPEN BOOK
3. SOPHOMORE	7. FRESHMAN	11. GIVE ME
4. PHILOSOPHY	8. ERASE BOARD	12. AGENT

CROSSWORD PUZZLE   *page 64*

PYRAMID PUZZLE   *page 61*

```
        M Y
      A C T
    C A N T
  Q U E R Y
 H E A L T H
L I B R A R Y
G R A D U A T E
```

Can't   Library   Act

Graduate   Health   My   Query

PHRASE PUZZLE   *page 63*

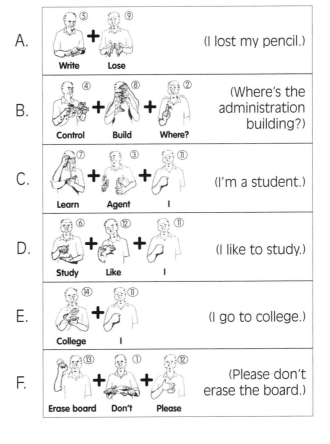

A. Write ⑤ + Lose ⑨   (I lost my pencil.)

B. Control ④ + Build ⑧ + Where? ②   (Where's the administration building?)

C. Learn ⑦ + Agent ③ + I ⑪   (I'm a student.)

D. Study ⑥ + Like ⑫ + I ⑪   (I like to study.)

E. College ⑭ + I ⑪   (I go to college.)

F. Erase board ⑬ + Don't ① + Please ⑫   (Please don't erase the board.)

CHAPTER 10

ALPHABET PUZZLE   *page 66*

① G R E A S E

②  C O R N

③ E A S Y

④ S E R V E

DEFINITION PUZZLE   *page 68*

 ① A. Apple / B. Peach / C. Orange

 ② A. Water / B. Milk / C. Juice

 ③ A. Whiskey / B. Wine / **C. Beer**

④ A. Bacon / B. Eggs / C. Sausage

 ⑤ A. Coke / **B. Pepsi** / C. 7-Up

 ⑥ A. Pickle / **B. Onion** / C. Relish

⑦ A. Deli / B. Diner / **C. Restaurant**

 ⑧ **A. Meat** / B. Fruit / C. Vegetables

⑨ A. Fork / B. Knife / **C. Spoon**

 ⑩ A. Small / **B. Medium** / C. Large

MATCH PUZZLE   *page 66*

① **Dessert** + ⑥ **Ice cream**

② **Coffee** + ⑧ **Cream**

③ **Salt** + ⑤ **Pepper**

④ **Bread** + ⑦ **Butter**

SCRAMBLE PUZZLE   *page 67*

①  S L A G S (GLASS)

② 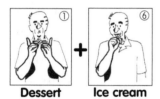 M N O E L (LEMON)

③ 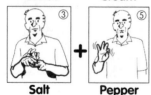 D A A L S (SALAD)

④  Y U L S O (LOUSY)

⑤ 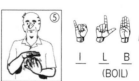 I L B O (BOIL)

⑥ 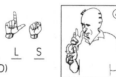 C H I H W (WHICH?)

⑦ 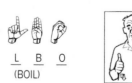 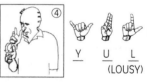 R A T O C R (CARROT)

⑧   E N W I (WINE)

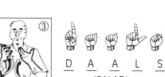      

SEARCH PUZZLE *page 70*

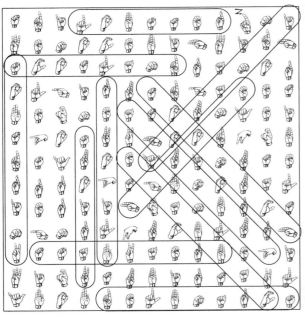

1. BREAKFAST
2. CABBAGE
3. FLIP OVER
4. ENOUGH
5. LOBSTER
6. SCOTLAND
7. SCRAMBLED
8. SOFT DRINK
9. THUMB UP
10. TOO MUCH
11. YOU AND I
12. VARIOUS

CROSSWORD PUZZLE *page 72*

PYRAMID PUZZLE *page 69*

W E T
F I S H
O R D E R
P O T A T O
L E T T U C E
C O C K T A I L
D E L I C I O U S

① Potato ② Wet ③ Order
④ Lettuce ⑤ Fish ⑥ Delicious ⑦ Cocktail

PHRASE PUZZLE *page 71*

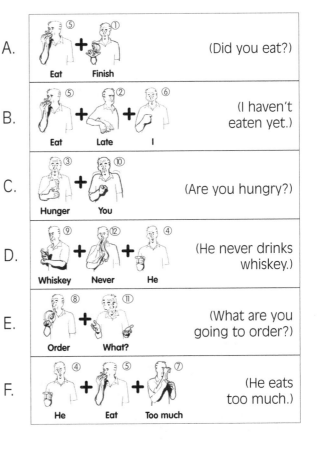

A. ⑤ Eat + ① Finish (Did you eat?)

B. ⑤ Eat + ② Late + ⑥ I (I haven't eaten yet.)

C. ③ Hunger + ⑩ You (Are you hungry?)

D. ⑨ Whiskey + ⑫ Never + ④ He (He never drinks whiskey.)

E. ⑧ Order + ⑪ What? (What are you going to order?)

F. ④ He + ⑤ Eat + ⑦ Too much (He eats too much.)

CHAPTER 11

ALPHABET PUZZLE   *page 74*

① S H O R T S

② M U S T

③ N I C E

④ A G R E E

DEFINITION PUZZLE   *page 76*

 ①
A. Shirt
B. Coat
C. Jacket

 ②
A. Never
B. Sometimes
C. Always

 ③
A. Who?
B. What?
C. Why?

 ④
A. Shouldn't
B. Can't
C. Won't

 ⑤
A. Day
B. Noon
C. Night

 ⑥
A. Wrinkled
B. Faded
C. Dirty

 ⑦
A. Some
B. A few
C. Most

 ⑧
A. Begin
B. Work on
C. Finish

 ⑨
A. Man
B. Woman
C. Child

 ⑩
A. Near
B. Rear
C. Here

MATCH PUZZLE   *page 74*

① **Shoes** + ④ **Socks**

② **Coat** + ⑧ **Tie**

③ **Blue** + ⑥ **Color**

⑤ **Wash clothes** + ⑦ **Washing machine**

SCRAMBLE PUZZLE   *page 75*

① Y A A S L W (ALWAYS)

② I R P (RIP)

③ A G B R (GRAB)

④ K C O S S (SOCKS)

⑤ T B L E (BELT)

⑥ T H R I S (SHIRT)

⑦ E A M S (SAME)

⑧ E W S (SEW)

SEARCH PUZZLE *page 78*

E	J	W	D	M	A	U	Q	G	N	A	R	W
A	V	E	N	A	C	N	A	U	P	Y	O	P
Q	U	E	X	E	A	Z	I	A	T	A	Y	J
V	U	R	E	L	I	M	N	J	E	D	L	W
S	K	C	A	L	S	T	M	O	D	Y	U	L
I	A	C	E	X	S	E	W	L	W	R	J	Q
W	A	L	M	E	E	R	N	O	W	E	W	U
I	D	E	A	R	W	O	E	R	B	V	E	R
G	W	A	S	H	C	L	O	T	H	E	S	I
E	F	N	E	Z	A	I	N	O	R	Z	G	I
E	Q	E	M	O	K	V	Y	O	U	O	W	H
D	U	R	I	N	G	H	E	U	Q	U	H	C
O	N	S	E	G	E	E	W	R	L	O	O	S

1. SHORTER SLEEVE	5. EVERY DAY	9. CAN
2. SLACKS	6. CLEANERS	10. DURING
3. WASH CLOTHES	7. HAVE	11. SAME
4. PANTS	8. NOW	12. BOW TIE

CROSSWORD PUZZLE *page 80*

PYRAMID PUZZLE *page 77*

		P	U	T		
	G	R	A	B		
A	G	R	E	E		
S	U	M	M	E	R	
T	I	E	K	N	O	T
O	P	P	O	S	I	T	E

Summer Opposite Put

Tie knot Grab Agree

PHRASE PUZZLE *page 79*

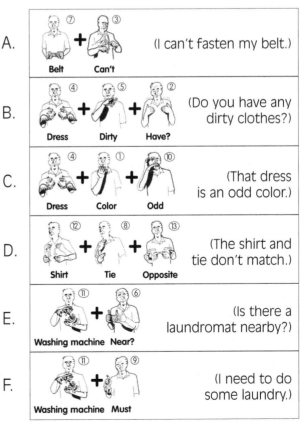

A. Belt + Can't (I can't fasten my belt.)

B. Dress + Dirty + Have? (Do you have any dirty clothes?)

C. Dress + Color + Odd (That dress is an odd color.)

D. Shirt + Tie + Opposite (The shirt and tie don't match.)

E. Washing machine + Near? (Is there a laundromat nearby?)

F. Washing machine + Must (I need to do some laundry.)

CHAPTER 12

ALPHABET PUZZLE *page 82*

① P E O P L E

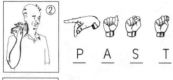
② P A S T

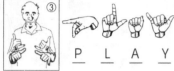
③ P L A Y

④ C A R D S

DEFINITION PUZZLE *page 84*

① A. Spring
B. Summer
C. Autumn

② A. Chess
B. Checkers
C. Dominoes

③ A. Chess
B. Checkers
C. Dominoes

④ A. Sailboat
B. Canoe
C. Kayak

⑤ **A. Summer**
B. Winter
C. Spring

⑥ A. Daily
B. Weekly
C. Monthly

⑦ A. Hiking
B. Hunting
C. Hockey

⑧ **A. Basketball**
B. Football
C. Volleyball

⑨ **A. Electronic games**
B. Board games
C. Field games

⑩ A. Strong
B. Muscular
C. Exercise

MATCH PUZZLE *page 82*

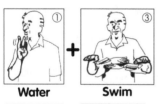
① **Water** + ③ **Swim**

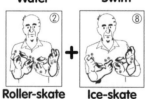
② **Roller-skate** + ⑧ **Ice-skate**

④ **Horse** + ⑥ **Ride horse**

⑤ **Olympics** + ⑦ **Compete**

SCRAMBLE PUZZLE *page 83*

① N E I N S T
(TENNIS)

② A C N
(CAN)

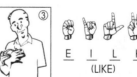
③ E I L K
(LIKE)

④ R E L A N
(LEARN)

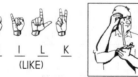
⑤ V O E L
(LOVE)

⑥ L I S K L
(SKILL)

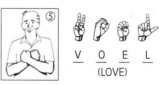
⑦ Y A M N
(MANY)

⑧ E H S
(SHE)

SEARCH PUZZLE *page 86*

CROSSWORD PUZZLE *page 88*

1. BOWL
2. FOOTBALL
3. CRAZY
4. DON'T LIKE
5. GO TO
6. DO WHAT?
7. WANT
8. TRY
9. PLEASE
10. TENNIS
11. REST
12. WHAT?

PYRAMID PUZZLE *page 85*

PHRASE PUZZLE *page 87*

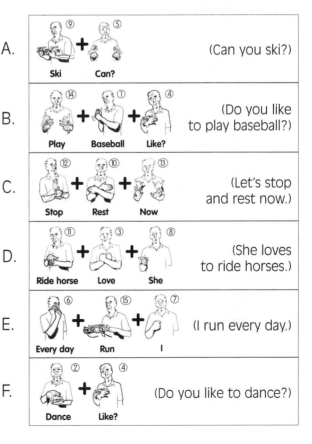

CHAPTER 13

ALPHABET PUZZLE   *page 90*

① P O L A N D

② S L O W

③ L E F T

④ H O T E L

DEFINITION PUZZLE   *page 92*

 ① A. Car
B. Train
C. Airplane

 ② A. Airplane take-off
B. Airplane flight
C. Airplane landing

 ③ A. License
B. Ticket
C. Passport

 ④ A. Canada
B. United States
C. Mexico

 ⑤ A. Ireland
B. Israel
C. Italy

 ⑥ A. Denmark
B. Sweden
C. Norway

 ⑦ A. Washington
B. New York
C. Chicago

 ⑧ A. Airplane take-off
B. Airplane flight
C. Airplane landing

 ⑨ A. Elevator
B. Escalator
C. Stairwell

 ⑩ A. Hungary
B. Hawaii
C. Holland

MATCH PUZZLE   *page 90*

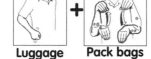
① Luggage + ⑦ Pack bags

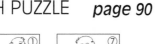
② Europe + ⑤ England

③ Stop + ⑧ Prohibit

④ Buy + ⑥ Ticket

SCRAMBLE PUZZLE   *page 91*

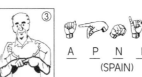
① O E N G T
(GET ON)

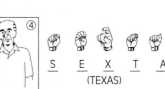
② C H W H I
(WHICH?)

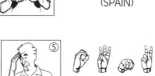
③ A P N I S
(SPAIN)

④ S E X T A
(TEXAS)

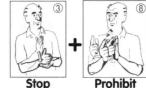
⑤ O W N K
(KNOW)

⑥ P A A N J
(JAPAN)

⑦ C R I F A A
(AFRICA)

⑧ H A B T
(BATH)

SEARCH PUZZLE   *page 94*

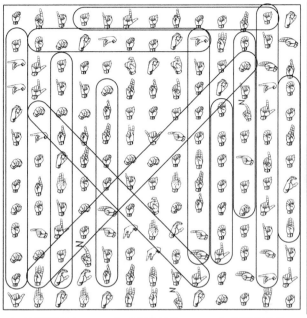

1. LEFT TURN
2. APPOINTMENT
3. LET'S SEE
4. BECAUSE
5. AUSTRALIA
6. CALIFORNIA
7. RIGHT TURN
8. PHILADELPHIA
9. POSTPONE
10. PITTSBURGH
11. MAGAZINE
12. WASHINGTON

CROSSWORD PUZZLE   *page 96*

PYRAMID PUZZLE   *page 93*

```
        S I T
      B E L T
    E G Y P T
  C A N A D A
A R I Z O N A
S T A Y H E R E
M I L W A U K E E
```

Arizona ① · Stay here ② · Egypt ③
Belt ④ · Canada ⑤ · Sit ⑥ · Milwaukee ⑦

PHRASE PUZZLE   *page 95*

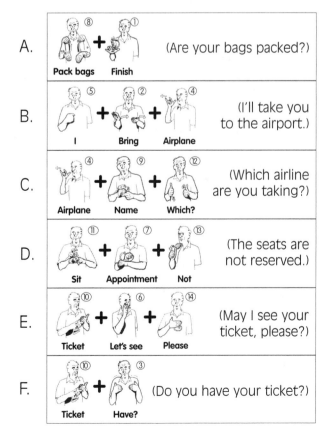

A. Pack bags ⑧ + Finish ① (Are your bags packed?)
B. I ⑤ + Bring ② + Airplane ④ (I'll take you to the airport.)
C. Airplane ④ + Name ⑨ + Which? ⑫ (Which airline are you taking?)
D. Sit ⑪ + Appointment ⑦ + Not ⑬ (The seats are not reserved.)
E. Ticket ⑩ + Let's see ⑥ + Please ⑭ (May I see your ticket, please?)
F. Ticket ⑩ + Have? ③ (Do you have your ticket?)

CHAPTER 14

ALPHABET PUZZLE *page 98*

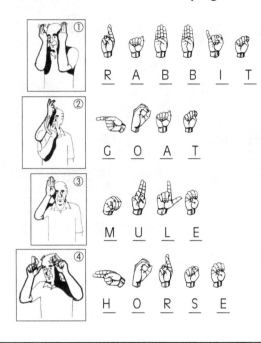

① R A B B I T

② G O A T

③ M U L E

④ H O R S E

DEFINITION PUZZLE *page 100*

   ①
A. Lion
B. Tiger
C. Cat

 ②
A. Clear
B. Dark
C. Hazy

③
A. Rooster
B. Turkey
C. Chicken

 ④
A. Gorilla
B. Monkey
C. Orangutan

 ⑤
A. Pink
B. Red
C. Purple

 ⑥
A. Mouse
B. Rat
C. Raccoon

 ⑦
A. Insect
B. Spider
C. Cockroach

 ⑧
A. Sheep
B. Bull
C. Goat

⑨
A. Moose
B. Deer
C. Caribou

⑩
A. Bird
B. Hawk
C. Chicken

MATCH PUZZLE *page 98*

① **Frog** + ⑧ **Green**

② **Tiger** + ⑦ **Orange**

③ **Bear** + ⑤ **Brown**

④ **Mouse** + ⑥ **Gray**

SCRAMBLE PUZZLE *page 99*

①
C A L K B
(BLACK)

②
E P E S H
(SHEEP)

③
W O R N B
(BROWN)

④
G E E A L
(EAGLE)

⑤
E B U L
(BLUE)

⑥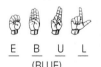
E I R T G
(TIGER)

⑦
T E N C I S
(INSECT)

⑧
M R W O
(WORM)

SEARCH PUZZLE   *page 104*

1. EAGLE
2. BLUE
3. CHICKEN
4. FROG
5. GREEN
6. LION
7. WHITE
8. RABBIT
9. SNAKE
10. MOUSE
11. TIGER
12. PINK

CROSSWORD PUZZLE   *page 102*

PYRAMID PUZZLE   *page 101*

Bird   **Animal**   **Butterfly**

Giraffe   **Dog**   **Elephant**   **Clear**

CHAPTER 15

ALPHABET PUZZLE *page 105*

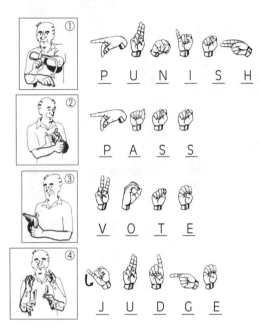

① P U N I S H

② P A S S

③ V O T E

④ J U D G E

DEFINITION PUZZLE *page 107*

① A. Cost
B. Lost
C. Crossed

② A. Too little
B. Too much
C. Too late

③ A. This year
B. Next year
C. Last year

④ A. Name
B. Same
C. Fame

⑤ A. Let
B. Get
C. Met

⑥ A. Petition
B. Protest
C. Punish

⑦ A. Disbelieve
B. Discount
C. Disobey

⑧ **A. Will**
B. Skill
C. Until

⑨ **A. All morning**
B. All afternoon
C. All night

⑩ A. Veto
B. Vote
C. Vex

MATCH PUZZLE *page 105*

① + ⑦
Picket   **Protest**

② + ⑧
Car   **Vehicle**

③ + ⑤
Pass   **Law**

④ + ⑥
Country   **City**

SCRAMBLE PUZZLE *page 106*

① B E A M Y
(MAYBE)

② K R E B A
(BREAK)

③ P R I A D
(RAPID)

④ R E G L A
(LARGE)

⑤ Y E O B
(OBEY)

⑥ R E N L A
(LEARN)

⑦ S T E E N A
(SENATE)

⑧ Y I T C
(CITY)

 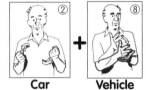 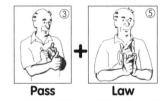 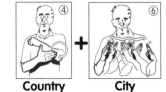          

SEARCH PUZZLE   *page 109*

```
L E S G I A M A Y B E T H
A N T D S K E E M I N O E
C N A C I L B U P E R Y R
E T A D V O U Q U E Z E B
B A N I E L S R S T E L C
R N N E E M D P U Q M T A
I A R C M O O R V U U H U
S L E A R N E C R U E Q S
H P D X S E R U R X U R E
L I A I N T H E I A T O Y
Y L B A P O R A V E T H E
E U U L A N G E O E W Y E
E Y U Q K A R O G A G U E
```

1. BECAUSE
2. DEMOCRAT
3. LEARN
4. GOVERNMENT
5. GO TO
6. PLAN
7. OBEY
8. REPUBLICAN
9. RAPID
10. MAYBE
11. RESPONSIBLE
12. WHO?

CROSSWORD PUZZLE   *page 110*

Across/Down grid:

¹S	U	P	P	O	R	³T		⁴J	U	D	⁵G	E
E			R		H		A				O	
C		⁶W	E		⁷P	E	T	I	T	I	O	N
O			S		Y		L				D	
⁸N	O	T	I	F	Y			⁹C				
D			D					A		¹⁰S		
¹¹A	R	R	E	S	T		¹²L	A	¹³R	G	E	
M			N					G		N		
O		¹⁴I	T		¹⁵W	O	M	A	N		A	
T					I			I			T	
¹⁶I	N	D	E	P	E	N	D	E	N	T	E	
O					S							
N		¹⁷L	E	G	I	S	L	A	T	U	R	E

PYRAMID PUZZLE   *page 108*

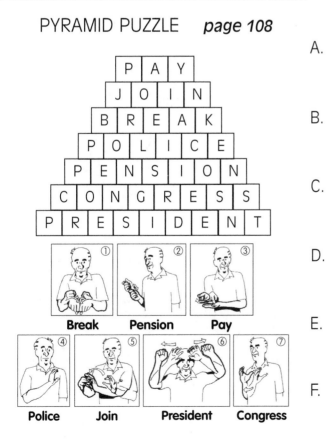

```
      P A Y
    J O I N
  B R E A K
  P O L I C E
 P E N S I O N
C O N G R E S S
P R E S I D E N T
```

Break ①
Pension ②
Pay ③
Police ④
Join ⑤
President ⑥
Congress ⑦

PHRASE PUZZLE   *page 112*

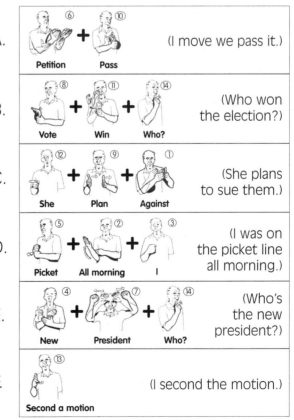

A. Petition ⑥ + Pass ⑩ — (I move we pass it.)

B. Vote ⑧ + Win ⑪ + Who? ⑭ — (Who won the election?)

C. She ⑫ + Plan ⑨ + Against ① — (She plans to sue them.)

D. Picket ⑤ + All morning ② + I ③ — (I was on the picket line all morning.)

E. New ④ + President ⑦ + Who? ⑭ — (Who's the new president?)

F. Second a motion ⑬ — (I second the motion.)

155

Answer Key
CHAPTER 16

ALPHABET PUZZLE *page 113*

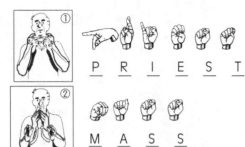

P R I E S T

M A S S

S O U L

A N G E L

DEFINITION PUZZLE *page 115*

① A. Agony / B. Against / **C. Again**

② **A. Music** / B. Minister / C. Mormon

③ A. Communication / B. Confession / C. Congregation

④ A. Annoint / B. Bless / **C. Worship**

⑤ A. Grave / B. Tombstone / **C. Funeral**

⑥ A. Friday / **B. Saturday** / C. Sunday

⑦ A. Cherish / **B. Church** / C. Choir

⑧ **A. Religion** / B. Resurrection / C. Rector

⑨ A. Heaven / **B. Hell** / C. Harp

⑩ A. Teach / B. Reach / **C. Preach**

MATCH PUZZLE *page 113*

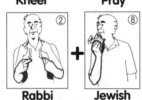
Kneel + **Pray**

Rabbi + **Jewish**

Believe + **Faith**

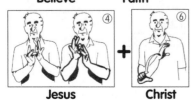
Jesus + **Christ**

SCRAMBLE PUZZLE *page 114*

① B R I B A (RABBI)

② V I D E L (DEVIL)

③ C U I S M (MUSIC)

④ R E V G A (GRAVE)

⑤ T A W N (WANT)

⑥ I F H A T (FAITH)

⑦ P E E L M T (TEMPLE)

⑧ O N J I (JOIN)

156

SEARCH PUZZLE *page 117*

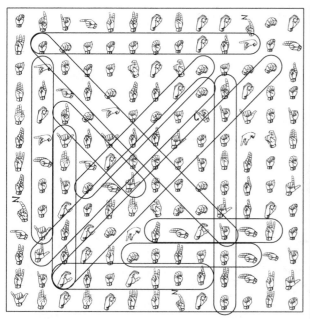

1. CONFESSION
2. CRUCIFY
3. CRACKER
4. DISBELIEVE
5. INTERPRET
6. HEAVEN
7. PROTESTANT
8. WHICH?
9. LUTHERAN
10. PROPHESY
11. MORMON
12. LORD

CROSSWORD PUZZLE *page 118*

PYRAMID PUZZLE *page 116*

PHRASE PUZZLE *page 120*

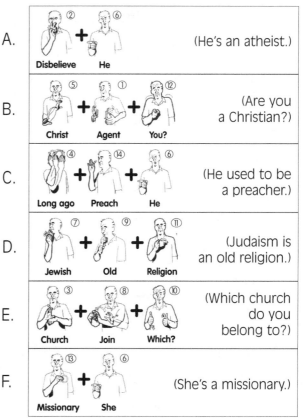

A. Disbelieve + He — (He's an atheist.)

B. Christ + Agent + You? — (Are you a Christian?)

C. Long ago + Preach + He — (He used to be a preacher.)

D. Jewish + Old + Religion — (Judaism is an old religion.)

E. Church + Join + Which? — (Which church do you belong to?)

F. Missionary + She — (She's a missionary.)

CHAPTER 17

ALPHABET PUZZLE   *page 121*

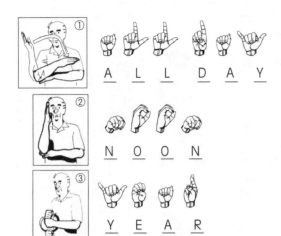

① A L L   D A Y

② N O O N

③ Y E A R

④ M O V I E

DEFINITION PUZZLE   *page 123*

①
A. **Birth**
B. Life
C. Death

②
A. 10,000
B. 100,000
C. **1,000,000**

③
A. Easter
B. Hanukkah
C. **Christmas**

④
A. **Than**
B. Then
C. Thin

⑤
A. Every Thursday
B. **Every Tuesday**
C. Every Friday

⑥
A. 10¢
B. **25¢**
C. 50¢

⑦
A. **Graduate**
B. College
C. University

⑧
A. **T-T-Y**
B. T-Y-T
C. Y-T-T

⑨
A. Summer
B. **Autumn**
C. Winter

⑩
A. Daily
B. Weekly
C. **Monthly**

MATCH PUZZLE   *page 121*

① **Dollar** + ⑦ **Money**

② **Time** + ⑥ **Afternoon**

③ **Buy** + ⑧ **Pay**

④ **Owe** + ⑤ **Broke**

SCRAMBLE PUZZLE   *page 122*

① N O H E P
<u>(PHONE)</u>

② T O M H N
(MONTH)

③ T H I G N
(NIGHT)

④ K R E B O
(BROKE)

⑤ E N N O
(NONE)

⑥ N E E R T
(ENTER)

⑦ M U R S E M
(SUMMER)

⑧ V E A H
(HAVE)

SEARCH PUZZLE   *page 125*

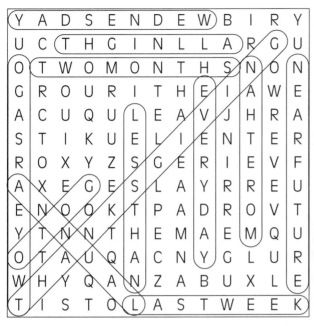

```
Y A D S E N D E W B I R Y
U C T H G I N L L A R G U
O T W O M O N T H S N O N
G R O U R I T H E I A W E
A C U Q U L E A V J H R A
S T I K U E L I E N T E R
R O X Y Z S G E R I E V F
A X E G E S L A Y R R E U
E N O O K T P A D R O V T
Y T N N T H E M A E M Q U
O T A U Q A C N Y G L U R
W H Y Q A N Z A B U X L E
T I S T O L A S T W E E K
```

1. EVERY DAY
2. ANNUAL
3. GO TO
4. LESS THAN
5. LAST WEEK
6. ALL NIGHT
7. WEDNESDAY
8. TWO MONTHS
9. NEAR FUTURE
10. THANKSGIVING
11. TWO YEARS AGO
12. MORE THAN

CROSSWORD PUZZLE   *page 126*

PYRAMID PUZZLE   *page 124*

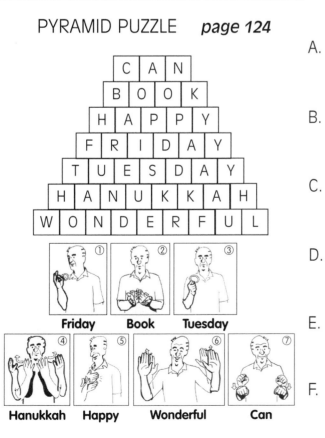

```
        C A N
      B O O K
    H A P P Y
  F R I D A Y
 T U E S D A Y
H A N U K K A H
W O N D E R F U L
```

Friday ①   Book ②   Tuesday ③

Hanukkah ④   Happy ⑤   Wonderful ⑥   Can ⑦

PHRASE PUZZLE   *page 128*

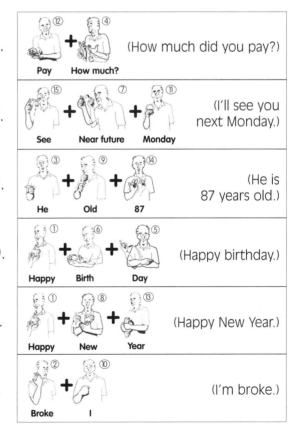

A. Pay ⑫ + How much? ④   (How much did you pay?)

B. See ⑮ + Near future ⑦ + Monday ⑪   (I'll see you next Monday.)

C. He ③ + Old ⑨ + 87 ⑭   (He is 87 years old.)

D. Happy ① + Birth ⑥ + Day ⑤   (Happy birthday.)

E. Happy ① + New ⑧ + Year ⑬   (Happy New Year.)

F. Broke ② + I ⑩   (I'm broke.)

159